T0112469

tidy the f*ck up
the american art of organizing your sh*t

messie condo

Racehorse Publishing

Racehorse Publishing books may be purchased in bulk at special discounts for sales promotion, corporate gifts, fund-raising, or educational purposes. Special editions can also be created to specifications. For details, contact the Special Sales Department, Sky Pony Press, 307 West 36th Street, 11th Floor, New York, NY 10018 or info@skyhorsepublishing.com.

Racehorse Publishing™ is a pending trademark of Skyhorse Publishing, Inc.®, a Delaware corporation.

Visit our website at www.skyponypress.com.

10 9 8 7 6 5

Library of Congress Cataloging-in-Publication Data is available on file.

Cover design by Brian Peterson
Cover artwork by Getty Images

Print ISBN: 978-1-63158-544-9
Ebook ISBN: 978-1-63158-545-6

Printed in the United States of America

Contents

Introduction   ix

1

Why Can't You Get Your Sh*t Together?   1

It's not that you don't know how, it's that
you don't want to   2

A tidying marathon will make you hate tidying   4

A little at a time is still something, so take the fucking win   6

Screw perfection—aim for happy   8

The only way to get what you want is to know
what that is   10

Dumping everything in bins won't help   12

Do what works for you—sort by room, category,
whatever!   14

You didn't accumulate all of this shit in a day   16

Your Chapter 1 Checklist   18

2

Throw Sh*t Out   21

Designate a purge and allow yourself to break some rules   22

Remember what your happy place looks like   23

Surround yourself with stuff you like and use   26

Does your enjoyment of the thing transcend logic?   28

The practical approach to joy   30

Resist the urge to multitask   32

Save the sentimental shit for later   34

Stay in your lane   36

You can't control other people   38

Your family doesn't want your shit   40

Turn off the fucking television   42

Be like Elsa and let it go   44

Aunt Mary won't notice if you donate her dishes   46

Storage units are a racket   48

Your Chapter 2 Checklist   50

3

How to Organize Your Sh*t   53

Getting down to brass tacks   54

Books   **56**

It's not a fucking trophy case   56

Get real—you're never reading that 58

Proudly display your "desert island" picks 60

Magazines get a special shout-out 61

Papers **63**

Your smartphone is your BFF 63

Get your inspiration from better sources 65

Reclaim the refrigerator 66

It's the 21st century: time for paperless statements 67

Have stereo instructions ever been useful? 68

If you didn't learn it the first time . . . 69

Don't leave the money stuff lying around 70

Random crap **71**

If it doesn't have a home, its home is in the trash 71

Your kitchen is full of random crap 74

How many fucking pens do you need? 75

Your bathroom should not look like an Ulta Beauty 76

No, you don't need an Ethernet cable 78

Ditch the DVDs (and Blu-Rays) 79

The American version of a savings account

(the piggybank) 80

Honorable mention: empty boxes 81

Clothing **82**

You have too many fucking sweaters 82

You're entitled to your sweatpants 85

A messy heap takes up more space than tidy items 86

If you can't see it, you won't wear it 87

It's a closet, not an Oreo—don't overstuff it 88

Life is too fucking short to fold your underwear 89
Where to put your parka in June 91
Memory Lane **92**
Carve out a day for this one 92
Resistance is futile 94
Don't confuse the memory with the thing 95
Keep the crème de la crème 96
Photographic memory not required 97
Collectibles: display them or dump them 99
When is enough enough? 100
Your Chapter 3 Checklist 101

4

Put Sh*t Away 105

Decide where you want things 106
You don't have a lack of storage, you have too much shit 108
Work smarter, not harder 110
Keep your shit to yourself 112
Lean into the lazy 113
Pulling out that bottom bin is a bitch 116
Channel your inner MacGyver . . . or not 117
Russian nesting dolls have their shit together 119
Changing handbags doesn't have to be its own project 121
American closets are not one-size-fits-all 123
If you can see it, it should make you happy 126
Embrace the embarrassing shit 127

Live like your mother-in-law's stopping by   129
Clutter in organization's clothing   131
Be grateful, not guilt-ridden   132
Your Chapter 4 Checklist   134

5

The Magical Feeling of Having Your Sh*t Together   137

Become a decision-making badass   138
Make room in your life for more good stuff   139
A clean space helps you hit the reset button   141
Tidying is like therapy you don't have to pay for   143
Sometimes you're going to regret tossing the toaster   144
Dress like you're ready to get your hands dirty   146
How do you want your home to feel?   148
Your home has to evolve with you   149
Whenever possible, give old things new life   151
Clutter messes with your shit   153
Don't let your shopping history repeat itself   155
Life after clutter   157
Your Chapter 5 Checklist   158

Introduction

> "That's all your house is—it's a pile of stuff with a cover on it. You see that when you take off in an airplane. You look down, and you see everybody's got a little pile of stuff. . . . That's all your house is. It's a place to keep your stuff while you go out and get more stuff!"
>
> —George Carlin

With the exception of a handful of super-organized people, we human beings are a fucking mess. If you're Type A and pretty content with your obsessive need to control everything, you're probably not reading a book on how to get your shit together. This book is for the rest of us lazy assholes who are starting to think that the mess isn't "fine."

You can't be in the "it's fine" place and tidy up. If you're in the "it's fine" place, you're sitting on the couch, watching *The Marvelous Mrs. Maisel* and ignoring the fact that you haven't seen the floor in a few months. No, you have to be so sick of your own bullshit that you can't stand it anymore.

You have to be ready to make a change, because you're going to have to roll up your sleeves and do some actual fucking work. Stubborn determination is the real magic. If you're not completely fed up, you'll surrender to the mess five minutes into the cleanup and end up back on the couch.

You've picked up this book because you want to make a change. Or you couldn't wrap your head around the advice in other books. Or you just wanted a laugh. Any which way, you're ready for better things.

Don't let anyone bullshit you into thinking you can transform your home and your life overnight. You didn't create this mess in a day, you're not going to clean it up in one. Unless you're a psychopath and have utterly no attachment to the things that you've bought. But more than likely, you're surprisingly attached to crap you don't even like, and you're going to need a little help letting go.

Your mess is a combination of stress, envy, emotional

baggage, and some high-level susceptibility to marketing. Untangling all that isn't easy, but it's worth it. Don't know where to start? Then you've come to the right place.

This book is part tidying advice, part foul-mouthed comedy special, and part therapy session. It's meant to help you create your happy place *on your own terms*. There is no one-size-fits-all strategy. Take the bits that help, leave the ones that don't. Read the book all at once, a little at a time as you need it, or both. It's entirely up to you. (I don't give a damn whether you actually follow through—it's not my mess.)

Getting your shit together isn't just about being able to find your car keys (although that's pretty fucking useful). It's about having a home that feels like coming up for air after a shitty day at work. The steps are simple: get rid of shit that doesn't make you happy, find a place for what's left, and stop buying shit you don't need.

You were hoping for a shortcut, right? Well, you're in luck. I happen to have one on me: be selfish. I'm not saying you should be an asshole to your family or hoard your treasures like Scrooge McDuck. I'm just saying that you need to get clear on what *you* want. Not what your mom wants or what your third-grade teacher wants. Just you.

All you're trying to do when you buy shit is make

yourself happy. You think that next pair of sneakers or shiny new kitchen appliance is going to make you feel better. And it does, for a minute. But then the high wears off and you have to get your next fix.

Instead of bouncing from one useless object to the next, take the time to think about what you want. What would make you happy? What does your perfect space feel like? Get clear on that, and you'll have no problem getting your shit together.

Don't get in your head about how much you'll have to give up to get there. Focusing on what to get rid of is a recipe for depression. And hoarding. Instead, focus on what lights you up. Surround yourself with that kind of stuff. (We'll deal with your Negative Nancy crap about being practical later.)

If you have a partner/kids/roommate, you may have to compromise down the line. But the starting line is the same: everybody gets clear on what makes them smile. Most of the time, this makes finding compromise in a shared space simpler. Sometimes, it reveals more pressing issues than a messy house (like when a sexy Princess Leia poster makes him happy, but it makes you want to divorce him).

My methods may not change your life, but they should help you get a handle on your shit in more ways than one.

Knowing what you really want is a superpower. It helps you not only conquer your home but also fend off all the bullshit life throws at you. Think I'm kidding? Read the book and see for yourself. I'm not going to give it all away in the intro. This is a Marvel superhero movie—you have to stick around until the end to get the whole story.

tidy the f*ck up

1

Why Can't You Get Your Sh*t Together?

It's not that you don't know how, it's that you don't want to

Organization isn't magic, it's work. When you work all day, you damn sure don't want to come home and do more work. And if you work at home (stay-at-home parents and caretakers obviously included), you probably just throw your hands up in surrender at a certain point because you're constantly surrounded by the mess and don't have the time or energy to deal with it. At the end of the day, you just need a fucking break.

I get it. We all get it. But exhaustion and overwhelm aren't the only roadblocks to getting your shit together. **When you get right down to it, human beings are just lazy.** The first step to recovery is admitting you have a problem, right? We all have a problem: we don't want to do one more thing than we absolutely have to.

And thanks to endless innovation (on the part of people who give just enough fucks to create technology that caters to their own laziness), we find new ways to be lazy every day. Don't feel like going out to eat? Open an app and order in. You don't even have to talk to another human! Can't be bothered to go shopping for your nephew's birthday present? Well hello there, free two-day shipping!

But unless you have the money to pay someone else to clean up after you, you can't lazy your way out of organizing. **And here's the secret: no professional organizer worth her salt will do the work for you anyway.** Not only will the organization not stick, but God forbid she throws out your favorite tee shirt from eighth grade and you Yelp her into oblivion.

If you're ready to work and need the emotional support of an expert (or a good, swift kick in the ass), then it's money well spent. But you're going to have to get your hands dirty either way. So you have to want it. Marie Kondo herself can't help someone who won't help themselves. **You have to decide you're sick of your own shit and that you're going to do something about it.**

The moral of the story is that you're never going to *feel* like it. But you're a grown-ass adult, so do it anyway. Commit to getting your shit together. At the end of the day, it's still a lazy person's goal. You're not running a 5K or curing cancer. Tidying up is a simple act of self-care, like meditation or a DIY pedicure (complete with pumice scrub). You may find the process a little uncomfortable, but the work is worth the result.

A tidying marathon will make you hate tidying

Can you think of anything worse than spending an entire weekend cleaning out your house? How about forcing yourself to do it at warp speed with no breaks just so you can finish it before starting your work week on Monday? Sound like fun?

Nope. That sounds fucking miserable. And in reality, it's not going to help you avoid ever having to tidy up again. Rebound is annoying, but it's also just life. Even if you give your shoes a cozy little home in the hall closet, you're still going to leave them in the middle of the living room more often than not. Because laziness.

So how do you avoid taking two steps back for every step forward? Do the fucking work. **Rebound isn't a result of tidying in dribs and drabs. It happens when you half-ass the work.** And you're certainly more likely to half-ass your organizing efforts if you're exhausted from marathon tidying.

Half-assing the work looks like throwing your crap in a closet or shoving it under the bed just so it's not in your face. The mess is still there, it's just haunting your closet now like the Ghost of Outlet-Shopping Past. You still have to deal with it at some point. (In case you were wondering, leaving the mess for someone else to clean up after you leave or die is a dick move. You made the mess, *you* clean it up.)

Doing the work means really looking at each and every item and taking the time to think about whether you need it and where might be the best place for it. Sometimes the best place for it is nowhere near your house. Letting that shit go and organizing what's left can be mentally and emotionally exhausting, which is why you'll need some downtime. Maybe some caffeine. Definitely chocolate.

Occasionally, like a swallow to Capistrano, something you've organized finds its way back to its original mess. Maybe you half-assed it, or maybe you just got it wrong. You're human. It happens. Don't beat yourself up—just try again. The more you do the work, the easier it will become, and the less often you'll have to do it twice. Chalk it up to the tidying learning curve.

With the amount of crap Americans amass every year, it's probably impossible to tidy in one go anyway. Don't waste your time worrying about doing the impossible. Do what you can, when you can. **As long as you're committed to getting your shit together, you'll get there.**

A little at a time is still something, so take the fucking win

Human beings are hardwired to want instant gratification. Imagine walking into the clusterfuck that is your kids' playroom and walking out of a perfectly organized space just a few hours later. Great, right?

Great if you're actually going to put in the work: gathering up everything that belongs in the playroom, fighting with your four-year-old over toys he hasn't touched in a year, sneaking those toys out of the house in the middle of the night, corralling what's left, and organizing it into a system both of you can enjoy. Sure, there's nothing like going full Tasmanian devil on a task and seeing the fruits of your labor sooner rather than later. But I'm exhausted just thinking about it.

And isn't instant gratification what got you into this mess in the first place? Your son *needed* that toy, and you needed to avoid a tantrum in the middle of Target. You can't really blame him—you *needed* that "But first, coffee" tee. (We'll deal with your ever-expanding tee shirt collection later.)

First of all, stop impulse-buying unnecessary shit. Second, lower your fucking standards. A perfectly clean and organized space is a win for you? Who are you, Martha Stewart? Time to find gratification in the little things.

The good news is that you already know how to do this. When you order something online, you don't get to enjoy the item right that minute. The gratification comes from pressing the "place your order" button and knowing your new meat thermometer is on its way. When you start dieting, you don't get washboard abs overnight (OK, or ever). The gratification comes from seeing that number on the scale go down a little bit every day. **If you can't stop and appreciate the little wins, you'll never make it to the big ones.**

So you get all of your kids' crap into one room and you're not stepping on Legos in the living room anymore. That's a win! You go through your overflowing tee-shirt drawer and pull out five to donate (and then actually take them to the box and donate them). Win! Every little bit brings you closer to a tidy room.

Of course, you don't want to feel like all you do is tidy up. Designate days on and days off. In my house, Thursday nights are sacred. The only thing on my to-do list is to sit my ass on the couch and watch three hours of ABC's finest programming—wine and popcorn optional.

Whether you want to go through your house like a

tornado, or you can only handle five minutes before you start spiraling about your spending habits, you do you. Don't get discouraged if you can't tackle everything at once. It all counts.

Screw perfection—aim for *happy*

Do we not have enough fucking pressure in our lives? Apparently, the inventors of social media felt we needed a little more motivation. Just when you thought you couldn't feel worse about yourself, your college bestie posts a picture of the Pinterest-worthy unicorn cupcakes she just "whipped up" for her five-year-old's bake sale. Where the hell does Becky find the time?

Then you scroll down and see pics of Sarah's perfectly coordinated farmhouse décor. You look around at your untamed mess and you're ready to throw in the towel before you even begin. Why even try, right? You're never going to be as perfect as they are.

Well, I have good news for you! **Perfection is bullshit.** People only show you what they want you to see: a carefully curated collection of moments meant to impress. And even if Becky didn't buy those cupcakes and Sarah didn't hire a designer (though they totally did), everyone's amazing at something. You included.

And when you think about it, perfection ain't so great anyway. Chrissy Teigen didn't win the hearts of more than 22 million Instagram followers because she's perfect (though if anyone is . . .). People follow her because she's *happy*. Her posts show her celebrating wins and laughing at goofs, and her joy is tangible through it all. And people eat it up with a Chrissy-Teigen-designed spoon, because happy is so much better than perfect.

In fact, when you say that something's perfect (and you're not throwing shade at Becky), you really mean that it makes you happy. That's the goal. **That's what you should aim for—whatever style of organization and cleanliness lights you up inside.** If you feel tense, you're thinking about someone else's perfect. Stop it, stalker. Get your own perfect.

Aiming for someone else's version of perfection is just begging to be disappointed because it means something different to everyone. We're usually too busy leaning over our classmate's shoulder to do our own work, but you need to define your own goal if you're going to meet it.

Your definition of perfect might be a gallery-style wall of your favorite family photos. Or it might be a closet full of complete, expertly coordinated outfits. Or a floor so clear of crap and dirty clothes that you can roll out your yoga mat on a whim. **You get to decide what your happy place looks like and how you're going to get there.**

The only way to get what you want is to know what that is

If you're like me, your answer to "What makes you happy?" might be "The hell if I know." Remember that hard work we talked about? This is where it starts. Sure, you might stumble sideways into happiness. (I do every time I walk through the aisles of Home Goods.) But knowing where you're going makes it a hell of a lot easier to get there.

How can you turn your home into your happy place? **The trick is to stop worrying about how things look and start noticing how they feel.** How do you want to *feel* when you wake up? When you come home? When you walk into your bedroom? Your bathroom? Think about all the nooks and crannies of your living space and how they make you feel now, then think about how you *want* to feel in them. If you're reading this book, the two probably don't line up.

You're human, so at some point the "shoulds" are going to creep into your daydream and start ripping it into tiny, unrecognizable pieces. "Aunt Karen gave me that vase, so I *should* keep it where she can see it when she visits." "I really *should* exercise more, so maybe I can make room for an elliptical." "I *should* make my space more unisex in case I get married." (You might think that last one's crazy, but it happens.)

Fuck the shoulds. It's enough already. We spend too much of our fucking lives trying to make everyone else happy. This is about *you*.* Don't worry about what others will think or whether your space will look good filtered and cropped into a square. Just focus on making yourself happy. If you eventually have to deal someone else in, you can make changes later.

So, back to your imaginary happy place. How does your home measure up right now? What can you do to help bring it in line with your vision? Take that mental picture and zoom in. Notice the details. You should get an

---

*If you live with other people and/or curmudgeonly dogs, you may *occasionally* have to compromise your vision. But if you're the one doing the heavy lifting around the house, they may *occasionally* have to suck it up. You know where you stand better than I do.

idea of what's working for you and what's working against you. Good. Now you have a rough plan of attack.

Later, when you're in the middle of tidying up and you're ready to say "fuck it" and find your way to a glass of sangria, break out that mental picture. **Remember what you're working toward and how much better you'll feel when you get there.** Maybe mull it over while sipping that glass of sangria. (Just the one, though. Drunken tidying might sound like more fun than sober tidying, but Sober You will have to clean up after Drunk You anyway. There are better ways for Drunk You to spend your time.)

Dumping everything in bins won't help

If you wanted to, you could probably sort everything in your house into a variety of lovely, colorful bins and have your home looking like a page out of *HGTV* magazine in no time. And, sure, you'll probably feel better about your mess for a little while. Until you have to pull out and dig through several of those bins to find the charger for your Dustbuster.

It seemed like a good idea at the time. How often do you use the Dustbuster anyway? Why wouldn't you store the charger in a bin? You were sure you could easily remember where you put it. But you put it in the bin with the electronics, not in the bin with the cleaning supplies, like you'd thought. And then you couldn't tell it apart from the dozens of other chargers you still have for things you've long since tossed. Just in case, you know?

Sound familiar? **The truth is, organizing only works if you've gotten rid of all the unnecessary shit that gets in the way of the necessary shit.** Just because you can store something doesn't mean you should. In an ideal world, you wouldn't have to dig *through* anything to find what you need.

Take that bin of cords, for example. Do you really need three printer cables, six iPhone chargers (two of which are frayed to hell), two A/C adapters, the cord for your old PS2, and three different lengths of Ethernet cable? Considering that your computer and printer both work on wi-fi, you can safely get rid of at least six of those cables right off the bat. Then ditch the busted iPhone cords and disperse the others between the places you need them—nightstand, purse, car, and desk. Suddenly, finding that Dustbuster cord isn't a Herculean task. (Hint: It's one of those A/C adapters.)

So getting rid of all the useless crap in your house is Step 1. Do not pass Go, do not collect $200 until you finish Step

1. In fact, Step 1 can help you with that $200. Sell your stuff online, at a garage sale, or to a thrift shop. One man's trash is another man's treasure, and getting paid has a way of helping you feel better about letting shit go.

Step 2 is organizing what's left in a way that's useful to you and fits within your overall vision for your home. Don't put shit away until you've really dealt with it. That's how you end up with five bins of miscellaneous crap shoved under your bed and no idea where you put your extra phone case.

Step 3, though, is the hardest. Stop. Fucking. Shopping. **Clutter is like a weed: if you don't get rid of the source, it just keeps coming back.** (The source is your addiction to buying shit you don't need, in case that wasn't obvious.) Before you buy something, really think about whether or not it's just going to add to the mess in the long run.

Do what works for you—sort by room, category, whatever!

Some organizing gurus say sorting by category is best, while others prefer sorting by room. I say, if you start with something that's really been pissing you off, you're more likely to enjoy the process of fixing it and develop some momentum. Is that clusterfuck you call a bathroom cabinet making your fingers itch? Or maybe the absurd number of throw blankets you own is driving you crazy. Whatever it is, go for it!

Everything else is up to you. Some people thrive on checklists and others like to go with the flow. **The only "right" way to organize your shit is just to *start* organizing your shit.** That's the hard part—deciding you're going to dig in and then actually doing it. If you use a one-size-fits-all approach, you're going to start resenting the work and give up. So don't worry about whether you're doing it right. Doing it is what matters.

Weighing your options? Well, cleaning by category (rounding up all like items in the house into a single pile) has the added benefit of shaming you into obeying the Cardinal Rule: stop buying shit you don't need. When you see your thirty-two vacation-themed tee shirts all sprawled out on the floor, you're a hell of a lot more likely to skip the souvenir shop on your next trip.*

---

*If you wear/enjoy/love-beyond-reason those touristy tees, by all means, keep on buying. But beware the line between a funny tradition and a waste of money and space. A sleek album of postcards might be the smarter choice.

Cleaning by location can still work, though. Let's say you start with the living room, gathering up all the crap that doesn't belong there. Shove that stuff in the room where it does belong, but don't worry about tidying it yet. When the living room looks great, it boosts your motivation to tackle the bathroom. By the time you get to your bedroom, it will contain all the stuff you've cleared out of the other rooms. **Then it's time to put your big girl pants on and deal with what is probably a very large pile of random crap.**

Either way, you're going to do the work and make some tough decisions. And that's exhausting enough. So skip the unnecessary restrictions on how you get to the finish line. If you make the rules unbreakable, you won't want to play. (Remember, Monopoly is boring as hell until you break the rules and pool your penalty payments under Free Parking.)

You didn't accumulate all of this shit in a day

Imagine plowing through your tidying to-do list in a weekend, effortlessly discarding all of the unnecessary objects in your life and organizing what's left until your home looks like the cover of a Container Store catalog. With the right methods and mindset, you and your newly perfected space can live happily ever after! And if you're buying that, I have some magic beans you can take off my hands for a very reasonable price.

Get a grip. You spent years amassing all of this clutter—you're not going to clean it up in a weekend. **But once you realize what a disaster your living space is, you have to make a concerted effort to get your shit together.** You can't just start putting your dirty clothes in the hamper instead of on the chair (which you assume is there but haven't been able to see for months) and hope the rest of the mess takes care of itself.

I stand by what I said before: do what you can when you can. But don't let that shit drag on for years. Look at your calendar and give yourself a realistic deadline. **Then force yourself to stick to your timeline by setting up a donation pickup with a local charity or buying permits for a yard sale.** Only an asshole would flake on a charitable organization or dash the hopes of old, retired men looking for used tools at bargain prices.

To avoid burnout, designate just one day a week leading up to your chosen date to really work on things, then reward yourself for your effort. (You can tidy more often if you want to, but you're going to feel pretty resentful if you work all week and then tidy all weekend.) So let's say you bust your ass on Saturdays, then treat yourself to Sunday brunch. Just make sure you work hard enough to earn it. Mimosas are for winners.

When you finally do get rid of that giant pile of random crap you didn't need, take a good, hard look at it. In fact, take pictures. Then print them out and hang them on the fridge to remind yourself why you don't need the electric tea kettle you just added to your cart online. You have a microwave. It does the same thing. That kettle *will* end up in the next discard pile, and you'll be out fifty bucks. **Learn your fucking lesson.**

....

Your Chapter 1 Checklist

* Admit that you have a problem, then get to fucking work
* Realize that only you can get your shit together
* Do the work whether you feel like it or not
* Give yourself a break (physically and emotionally)
* Love the little wins

* Picture a happier living space and how you can make it happen
* Tell anyone who says "should" to fuck off—even you
* Make a list of what's working for you and what flat-out isn't
* Get specific about what you want your spaces to feel like
* Fight the urge to dump your shit in bins
* Get rid of shit you don't need, want, or like
* Give yourself a firm but forgiving deadline
* Treat yo'self for busting your ass

2

Throw Sh*t Out

Designate a purge and allow yourself to break some rules

When you're finally ready to face your mess and start tossing stuff into the discard pile, those pesky shoulds are going to pop into your head again. Guilt is a powerful deterrent—just ask your grandmother. But you need to call bullshit on guilt and reclaim your space.

When you think *But I spent so much money on that*, follow it up with *That'll teach me* and toss it in the bin. Can't part with the figurine Great Aunt Ida gave you for your eighth birthday, even though you're terrified of clowns and the thought of it haunts you from deep within a box in the basement? Nope! Out it goes. (In fact, throw that one in the trash. No one wants that shit.)

You might find it helpful to do one big purge, going through the house inch by inch and ousting anything that bugs you. Don't get in your head about it and waste time on the maybes. Just throw them in their own pile to deal with later. Doing a clean sweep like this can help you build up those "fuck it" muscles and let go of the guilt more easily. *Then* you tackle the maybes.

Sometimes you're lucky enough to wake up ready and raring to go. Other times, you just need to suck it up and start in. Trust me: you'll start to get into it as your discard pile grows. Just don't stop to organize until you finish culling the herd. You need to have a one-track mind if you're going to maintain your "fuck it" momentum.

Remember your goal: a home filled with only the things you love and use. Think of it like Michelangelo thought about his statue of David: he said that he didn't create David from the marble, he just chipped away at the marble to free an already existing David. (OK, so that story is probably crap. But it's relevant crap.)

You're not just getting rid of shit for the sake of it. You're chipping away at everything that doesn't contribute to the life you want for yourself. If you stop buying shit you don't need, you won't have to do it more than once. But who are we kidding? You'll probably need to make it a semi-annual event.

Remember what your happy place looks like

It's time for you to break out that mental picture of your endgame and get specific about what you want. A few pages ago, I told you to focus on how you want to feel rather than how you want your home to look. If that seemed a little woo-woo to you, it might be because you need a new perspective on your living space.

George Carlin was right—we treat our homes like containers for our stuff. But it's called a *living space* for a reason. Your home should not only reflect who you are but also help you live the way you want to live.

Still too earthy-crunchy for you? **Let's put it this way: stop treating your house like a fucking storage unit.** You *live* there! You spend, presumably, a shit ton of time there. It's where you start and end most of your days. When work sucks and people are pissing you off, don't you want to come home to a little oasis of your own making? Of course you do. So stop fucking resisting.

Your living room should be a place you look forward to hanging out in. Your bedroom should make you feel comfortable and relaxed. Your kitchen should make it easy to whip up your favorite foods. That's all going to mean something different to everyone reading this, so you have to dig deep and figure out what it means to you. What do *you* want?

Since so much of our lives is about pleasing other people, you're probably not used to thinking about what *you* want. Take your time with it. Savor the crazy ideas that pop into your head. There's always a way to incorporate even a little bit of the outlandish.

Maybe you want a reading room, complete with leather armchairs and floor-to-ceiling bookshelves. What if you pare down your clothing enough to fit it all in the closet, get rid of the extra dresser, and turn that space into a reading nook? **Anything's possible—it's just a matter of prioritizing what's important to you.**

Still have no idea what that might be? Spend some time on Pinterest or thumbing through home décor magazines. Make note of anything that makes you smile or light up. Again, it's not about what things look like, it's about how they make you feel.

So if you live in a studio apartment and you're drooling over a huge open kitchen, maybe it's not the kitchen itself that's calling your name. Maybe it's the feeling of spaciousness. Think about what you can do to make your current space feel that way. (If it's spaciousness you're looking for, not covering every surface with clothing in various states of cleanliness might be a start.)

Once you're really clear on what you want and why you want it, you'll be chomping at the bit to get your shit together. It's exactly the motivation you need to get the job done.

Surround yourself with stuff you like and use

We're all just dragons guarding our treasure, but we need to be way more fucking selective about what we call treasure. (However shiny, your third-grade trophies probably don't count.) **The concept is simple enough: get rid of all the shit you don't like or use, and keep the stuff you do like and use.** But people aren't simple, and you're bound to get in your own way.

You made this mess. You lovingly (or frantically, or begrudgingly) chose each and every component of it. This mess is yours. And once you mentally brand something *yours*, it becomes that much harder to let it go. So how do you stack the deck in your favor? *Ding, ding, ding!* You focus on what makes you happy. Now you're getting it!

If you've been following along like a good little reader, then you've taken the time to figure out what that is. That makes this part a little easier. Remember Michelangelo: getting rid of shit isn't the goal, it's the means to the end. **You're carving out space for the stuff you actually like and use—and only that stuff.**

With that in mind, spend a minute with every single thing in your house. (Those minutes add up, so clear your

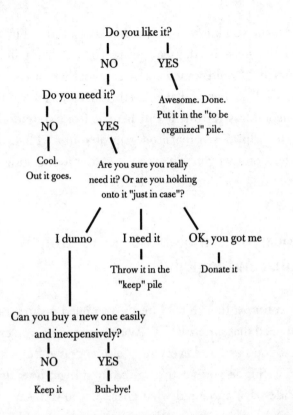

Do you like it?

NO — Do you need it?

YES — Awesome. Done. Put it in the "to be organized" pile.

Do you need it?

NO — Cool. Out it goes.

YES — Are you sure you really need it? Or are you holding onto it "just in case"?

I dunno — Can you buy a new one easily and inexpensively?

I need it — Throw it in the "keep" pile

OK, you got me — Donate it

Can you buy a new one easily and inexpensively?

NO — Keep it

YES — Buh-bye!

calendar for the afternoon and get comfortable.) Think about whether each thing fits your vision. **Ask yourself three questions: Do I like it? Do I need it? Can I buy a new one if I need to?** If you're not quite sure, refer to the handy-dandy flowchart above.

Maybe you know you don't like it or need it, but you're still having a hard time letting go. At that point, ask yourself, "Could someone else get more use or enjoyment out of it?" Knowing that your stuff isn't going to waste and someone less fortunate will benefit from your donation might help loosen that iron grip of yours. (That, or the realization that you're a greedy hoarder for hanging on to something you don't like or use.)

Does your enjoyment of the thing transcend logic?

Do you *need* that shirt? I mean, you need *a* shirt. But do you need that *specific* shirt? At a certain point, you exceed what you need and everything else is gravy. But it's *your* gravy. So, as you go through your things, how do you decide what stays and what goes? If you've been paying attention, you know that the stuff that stays should fall into two categories: like and need. Let's focus on like first.

Hold that vintage Led Zeppelin tee shirt in your hands and ask yourself, "Does this vintage Led Zeppelin tee shirt spark joy?" If your answer is "I have no fucking idea," you're not alone. A lot of us are bumfuzzled by the idea of tapping into our intuition. So we might need to reframe the question in a more practical light. How about this: Do you *like* your vintage Led Zeppelin tee shirt?

Let's be clear. **When I ask you if you like something, your answer had damn well better not be, "Sure." This isn't the time or place for that lukewarm shit.** You don't need to be over the moon about every little thumbtack, but you do need to seriously consider whether each object in your home makes you happy. Does it put a smile on your face when you hold it/use it/look at it across the room? Do you *like* it?

Bonus points if you have no fucking clue *why* you like it. That means you're catapulting yourself past all logic and obligation. You're ignoring the shoulds and focusing on what makes you and you alone happy. That's the goal. That's the special sauce. If you think *I have no idea why I love this so much, but I do*, then it's a keeper. Screw the practical use.

Maybe you have what it takes to tear ruthlessly through your belongings and proclaim them all goners. More likely, you're going to start second-guessing yourself about three tee shirts in. All of those shoulds start piling up: "I like it enough." "I loved it when I bought it." "I might need this for an interview/wedding/funeral/third cousin's baby shower." Suddenly, you have a closet full of *meh*.

Here's a handy trick: The first time you come across something that you love beyond reason, leave it out where you can see it. Use this beloved belonging as a barometer whenever you're having trouble deciding on something. **If you compare something that's meh to something you're crazy about, you're going to feel like an idiot for keeping it.** You have plenty of time to find something awesome to wear to the baby shower.

The practical approach to joy

OK, smart ass. I know what you're thinking. *My hair dryer doesn't make me happy. Should I throw it out?* You know what? Maybe.

It's true, surrounding yourself with things you love isn't always practical. Does a toilet plunger spark joy? Of course not. But you're going to be pretty fucking sorry if you don't have it when you need it. That doesn't mean that necessities can't also make you happy.

If you go around your home, I'll bet you can't name more than three items that don't have the *potential* to make you happy. Toilet paper? Maybe you're buying the wrong stuff, but my three-ply makes me happy. Pillows? If you don't look forward to laying your head down at night, you seriously need to spend some time at Bed Bath & Beyond. How about that hair dryer? Have you seen the colors those things come in? One of them is bound to put a smile on your face.

You can find plenty of ways to upgrade boring basics into something that fits your vision. Buy the colorful paperclips covered in polka dots instead of the plain ones. Spring for the fancy toaster that looks like an Easter egg. Trade in your wire hangers for soft, teal microfiber ones. Spray paint your filing cabinet hot pink if it will make you giggle every time you look at it. The list goes on and on.

Obviously, you don't want to go into hock to support your newfound tidying habits. **But small upgrades can make a big difference in how you feel in your home.** If you don't have the scratch, make the changes little by little. You already know you're not finishing this project in a weekend, so you have plenty of time to figure out which items you should swap. Maybe turn the upgrades into your reward for finishing parts of your tidy-up project.

For some people, knowing that something is necessary is enough to make them happy to keep it. The trick is to know the difference between actual necessity and "but I might need it someday." Refer back to that handy flowchart on page 27. Very few things are worth keeping "just in case." One little black dress or snazzy suit—fine. An entire wardrobe of fancy work clothes when you freelance from home in your pajamas—seriously? You know better. Just make your damn hands do what your brain knows they should and get rid of that shit.

Resist the urge to multitask

Like fast fashion and the incessant desire to accumulate shit we don't need, the urge to multitask is a uniquely 21st-century problem. It starts young, with TV and video games. Thirty-second commercial breaks and leveling up made you eager to move on to the next thing. Then you got older and overloaded with homework and extracurriculars. Next thing you know, you're an adult and are expected to do the work of twelve people in the span of a 40(ish)-hour workweek.

What I'm saying is that it's not entirely your fault that you can't sit still for two fucking minutes and organize your junk drawer. You're just not built for it. Unless you've mastered meditation, this part is going to be hard. You're going to have to focus on one thing at a time.

Did you just scream? Or collapse in despair? Or cry? No judgment—all are acceptable reactions to being asked to rewire your own brain. But if you flip back a few pages, you'll remember that a sense of accomplishment keeps you motivated. **If you put out a hundred tiny fires all over the house, you'll be exhausted and have precious little to show for it.**

Let's say, for example, you're in the middle of organizing your clothing and you notice a stray book. You'll be tempted to deal with it, mostly because that one book is a lot less intimidating than the heap of clothes on your bed. But if you've already organized the books, that stray begs a decision. And now you're distracted by your bookshelves and you have no place to sleep tonight because you didn't finish sorting your fucking clothes. Nip that shit in the bud and set the book aside until you're finished with Fashionista Mountain.

If you're someone who needs the challenge of multitasking to function, try this: set a timer for ten minutes and race the clock. Didn't finish your whole project in ten minutes? Shocking. Reset the timer and go again. When you're competing against time and doing the actual work, your brain will be too busy to ping-pong between unnecessary distractions.

If you're still having trouble staying on task, start with a really doable discarding project—something like clearing out old cleaning supplies. From start to finish, focus only on that task. After a short time, you should have a cupboard neatly stocked with only the products you like and use and a bin of extras to give to a local charity that really needs them. Roll that triumph into a slightly bigger project, building up your straightening stamina as you go.

Just don't forget to take breaks in between projects. You're not Deepak Chopra—you have only so many minutes of real focus in you.

Save the sentimental shit for later

Assuming you're not a monster, you're going to want to pore over old letters and photos and grapple with what to toss. Does that sound like a good use of your time when you're trying to get your shit together? No. **So carve out some hours (or days) in the future to deal with the feels.**

Think you can handle it? You can't. There's a reason you have bins and bins of shit from your childhood. Those mementos aren't just things, they're part of who you are. At least that's what you'll tell yourself when trying to clear them out. So instead of properly sorting through your past, you'll waste hours of your life only to shove it all back into bins and lock it away in an attic. A few years later, maybe you'll try again. Nothing will change.

Maybe it's worse than that. Maybe you're one of those people who let their parents enshrine their childhood bedroom instead of turning it into a home gym or Airbnb rental. Don't be the guy who can't let his parents move on with their lives. Deal with your shit. (Not now, though. Later. When you know what the hell you're doing. You're not nearly ready for that minefield.)

The truth is, those mementos really are just things. Someday, you'll look at that tee-ball participation trophy, enjoy the memory of the summer you realized you hate team sports, and then throw the useless thing out. But you need to be ready. You need to build up those "fuck it" muscles with the stuff you don't give a damn about. Eventually, you can work your way up to low-key childhood trauma.

Keep in mind, not all of your keepsakes are boxed. You're bound to come across a few while working on other projects—a photograph stuck in a book, or a figurine tucked on a shelf. When you're in the tidying zone, these items are kryptonite. Don't pause, don't look, and for fuck's sake, don't reminisce. Next thing you know, you'll have lost four hours of your life and accomplished nothing. Avert your eyes and throw it in the "later" pile.

When you're finished overhauling the rest of your home, break out those bins. (By now, you better have told Mom and Dad to take back their space and box up your shit for you to pick up. Don't even think about making them mail it.) With an arsenal of badass tidying skills, you'll be ready to see your childhood kitsch for what it is— taking up valuable space you could use for a Peloton bike.

Stay in your lane

Not everyone is going to be on board with your getting rid of half of your worldly possessions. That's fine. Maybe they'll get there eventually. Maybe they'll be featured on a future episode of *Hoarders*. Either way, you don't need their fucking permission. And you definitely don't need their shoulds piled on top of your own.

The road to hell (and *Hoarders*) is paved with the good intentions of loved ones who feel guilty about getting rid of stuff. Unless they own stock in your baseball card collection, they don't get a say in your discard decisions. "Oh, you're getting rid of that? Are you sure?" You're damn right I'm sure, Susan. Mind your own business.

You've already done the work and made the tough decisions. You're exhausted, but you're also excited to move on to the next section. Things are starting to shape up. The last thing you need is Susan making you second-guess yourself. To avoid shared guilt and hurt feelings, it's probably best for everyone if you keep your tidying to yourself. Don't let others in while you work, and don't let them see the donation boxes.

The rare exception is a good friend who will call you on your shit but who doesn't talk you into things you'll regret. This is someone who's supportive of the cause, who isn't a Spartan or a squirrel, and who has zero interest in going home with parting gifts. **If you're lucky enough to have people like this in your life, enlisting their help can turn the chore of tidying into a celebration of finally getting your shit together.**

Don't have any friends like that? Fuck it. Make it a solo celebration. Put on your favorite playlist, grab a glass of wine, and enjoy the hell out of creating the life you want. Notice I said *a* glass. One. No one wants to wake up with a hangover and realize they accidentally put their fancy electric toothbrush in one of seven sloppily packed donation boxes. (At that point, you should just donate whatever's in the boxes and buy a new toothbrush.)

What about those of you whose whole family is participating in the "get your shit together" challenge? You can't possibly tell your husband to mind his own business, right? Of course you can. Your books, your papers, your clothing, your kitsch—it's all *your* problem. His crap is his problem. You can have an opinion about that disgusting lucky jersey of his, but you don't get a vote. Keep your eyes on your own paper and tell him to do the same. When all is said and done, you both get to enjoy a cleaner, calmer living space.

You can't control other people

Once you get in the swing of discarding all of the crap you don't need and you start to see results, you're going to feel exhilarated. You're going to want to share that feeling with others, to spread the joy. Plus, it couldn't hurt to have some likeminded people around when you get to the hard stuff.

Remember me saying that you have to *want* to get your shit together? That no one else can help you if you won't help yourself? See where I'm going with this? **You can't make your mom/husband/kids/roommate want to get their shit together either. You can only control you.**

Let me be clear: that doesn't mean that you go around common areas, tidying up for them. You know what's a really bad idea? Throwing away another person's shit. I don't know if you've noticed, but people are pretty fucking possessive about their stuff. They chose it, they spent the money on it, it's theirs, for better or worse.

Think it through: You notice a pair of your husband's old sneakers living in the hall closet that you've never actually seen him wear and you say, "I'm just going to toss these in with my donate pile." Is that the hill you want to die on? Smelly old sneakers?* Because he's going to notice they're gone, and he's going to be pissed at you.

It doesn't matter if those sneakers went untouched for years. That's not the point. The point is they're not yours. You don't know what those sneakers mean to him. To you, they're just sneakers. To him, they're the sneakers he always wore when walking his old Black Lab, Duke, before he died.

See what you did? You threw away his dog, asshole.

---

*Don't be a dick. Wash your stuff before you donate it.

OK, so that's an extreme example. But you see what I mean. **You don't know why people have the stuff that they have, so mind your own tidying business and let others mind theirs.**

Most of the time, people will see how much happier you are with a clean slate and follow your good example. Human beings are simple creatures—we learn by observing, and we're easily influenced. (Just think about how long it took you to get McDonald's after seeing their last commercial. Monkey see, monkey do.) Instead of trying to force the people in your life to comply, teach them that tidy feels good.

Your family doesn't want your shit

Throwing shit out forces you to take personal responsibility for your choices. Yes, you chose to buy that as-seen-on-TV mini elliptical. Yes, you spent good money on it. Yes, it was a stupid decision that you now regret because you are lazy as fuck and will never choose exercise over sitting on the couch. You now have to own that bad decision, accept that you wasted the money, and send that useless thing packing.

The good news is that just because it's useless to you

doesn't mean it's useless to everyone else. Someone out there will love that mini elliptical (probably). You could try selling it through an app to recoup your cost. Or you could offer it to that friend who can't sit still long enough to read a book jacket. You could even donate it to a worthy charity that will resell it, benefitting both the charity and the new owner.

You know what's not an option here? Forcing your crap on people who don't want or need it in order to alleviate your own guilt. That doesn't make you charitable or resourceful. It makes you an asshole.

Sure, you *can* guilt your parents into taking some of your childhood keepsakes. And you know your brother can't say no to a freebie—his house is brimming with other peoples' hand-me-downs and discards. Before you know it, you'll have found new homes for all your unwanted crap without having to take any personal responsibility at all!

That's a big, fat *nope*. You got into this to ease your overwhelm and create a lasting space that makes you happy. How does bogging down your already-anxiety-riddled brother accomplish that? It doesn't help him, and it doesn't help you. In order to maintain your newly tidy surroundings, you need to learn your fucking lesson about accumulating crap you don't need.

There's nothing worse than knowing that you wasted your money and contributed to overflowing landfills. But you need to feel that if you're going to get your shit together *and* keep it together. **You have to own your mess.**

If you know your brother was shopping around for a down comforter, and you have a really good one that you don't need, go ahead and ask. But be prepared to take no for an answer and donate the thing. And remember, this road goes both ways. When someone else is ready to get their shit together, and they ask, "Do you want this old toaster?" the answer is no. Put your fingers in your ears and sing "La Bamba" if you have to. If you didn't need it before, you don't need it now.

Turn off the fucking television

If you're going to tackle that mountain of mess you've created, you'll need all the help you can give yourself. First, carve out time to devote to tidying—preferably when you're not exhausted by life. That means catering to whatever circadian rhythm works for you. If you're a morning person, tackle the tidying after coffee. If your brain starts firing on all cylinders at 10 o'clock at night, that's when you dive in. That way, you maximize your most productive time.

Second, I'm sorry, but you have to turn off the fucking television. Between cable, DVR, and streaming, most of us spend more time watching TV than we care to admit. We're so used to multitasking that we keep it on even when we're not really watching it. You just feel so much more productive if you can say that you folded laundry *and* watched *Grace and Frankie*,* right?

But sorting through your life one item at a time requires a little more attention to detail than folding your socks. You can't find the tidying flow if you're half-watching a rerun of *Friends*. If you're like me, you start out with the TV "on in the background." At some point, you sit down "just for this scene." Suddenly you're fully engrossed in *The One Where Ross and Rachel Take a Break* and you've lost your tidying mojo. Honestly, you won't even notice the TV's not on when you're tackling piles of crap like a boss.

---

*Frankly, *Grace and Frankie* deserves your undivided attention—and maybe a margarita. Save the laundry for *The West Wing*. You've seen every episode sixteen times. You don't even have to look up to know Toby's about to tell Sam not to "tempt the wrath of the whatever from high atop the thing."

Don't get me wrong—a little distraction can be a good thing. If you tend to hem and haw, it might help you get out of your head and make decisions more quickly. But you need to recognize when you're getting too distracted (like when you're dancing around the room, singing Meghan Trainor songs into a flashlight you just found at the back of your closet). A jaunty classical guitar riff might work better for you.

You might be tempted to take advantage of the TV-free time and listen to your favorite podcast or a new audiobook. You'll have to be the judge of whether that works for you, but my guess is that it won't. Not if they're any good, anyway. **The goal here is simple: take advantage of what motivates you and stay the fuck away from the things that drain your attention like an iPhone 6 battery.**

Be like Elsa and let it go

At some point, you're going to be elbow-deep in your clean-out and start to wonder why you ever thought you could part with the tennis racket your mom bought you in tenth grade. Never mind that you hated tennis (and the people who played it). Your mom bought it for you. Never mind that she knew you hated tennis before she bought it. It was a gift. From your mom. Whom you love.

Notice anything fishy? That's called rationalizing. And there's no fucking place for it in the middle of your discard phase. The whole point of focusing on whether something makes you happy is to leapfrog over that part of your brain. In tenth grade, it was about what your mom wanted. Now it's about what you want. Do *you* want a tennis racket? That's what I thought.

Don't overthink it. Don't let that sneaky little bit of uncertainty tug at your heartstrings and talk you into keeping shit you don't need or want. **If it's not a yes, it's a no.** And that's OK. Whether or not someone gave it to you. Whether or not you spent money on it. Whether or not you were crazy about it when you bought it. It's OK to oust half of your belongings if they don't work for you anymore. Seriously.

Accept when something's served its purpose, even if its purpose only lasted for the five minutes it took to bring it up to the register and check out. When the only reason to keep something is because you feel guilty getting rid of it, repeat after me: "Fuck it." **Be grateful you had the thing when you needed or wanted it, and then let that shit go.**

A fatal mistake is taking one last look at what you're getting rid of. If something didn't make it into your "keep" pile, it gets tossed. No second guessing yourself. You've already done the hard part: you've dug through everything and made a conscious decision about whether it's what you want. You're so close to being done. What do we say? "Fuck it." Trust yourself and tape up those boxes.

The last 10 percent of your effort is physically taking the stuff that didn't make the cut out of your house and on to its next destination. You get absolutely no points for boxing it up and letting it sit in your garage or your car just in case you change your mind. There is no fucking "just in case." The stuff goes. Imagine the relief you'll feel when those trash bags and donation boxes are out of your life. Embrace it!

Aunt Mary won't notice if you donate her dishes

One of the hardest things to give up is a gift, especially when you like the giver and know how much thought went into the gift. But the same rules apply: love it or lose it. You're a person. You contain multitudes. You can both be grateful for a gift and want to throw it into oncoming traffic at the same time.

First of all, a gift is yours to do with as you please. You could set it on fire in your backyard if you wanted to. (Please don't set it on fire.) Secondly, you would never want a friend or relative of yours to keep a gift you gave them out of guilt. Give yourself the same courtesy.

Finally—and this is the important part—the gift has already served its purpose. The giver has carefully selected it, packaged it, given it to you, and seen the joy on your face when you received it. They don't need to know you were smiling through gritted teeth. The truth is, they're probably not even going to remember what they gave you six months from now.

Think about it. Can you name all of the gifts you gave people for Christmas last year? Can you name all of the gifts you were given? My guess is that you're fuzzy on at least a few of them. That's because the real gift is the interaction between giver and recipient. Someone cared enough to buy you a gift, and in that moment, you really appreciated the thought. (At least you should have. If you didn't, try not to be such a dick going forward.)

The exception is the expensive or irreplaceable gift, which usually comes in the form of a family heirloom. That might be more about the gift itself than the interaction. But if you really can't stand the thing, you're still better off getting rid of it. Great Aunt Mary's dishes aren't doing anyone any good sitting in a padded storage case in the basement.

The best option is to give the dishes back to Aunt Mary. Tell her you just don't have a place for them and you don't want them to go to waste. She'll probably be grateful for your honesty and be happy to give them to someone who really wants them.

The bottom line is, if someone really loves you, they just want you to be happy. They certainly wouldn't want you to keep their ugly dishes if you didn't like them. And if keeping something you don't like really is that important to them, maybe pleasing them shouldn't be quite so important to you. You know what I'm saying? If Emily Gilmore had told her mother-in-law to fuck off when she complained about her "gifts" sitting in storage, she'd have been a much happier person for it.

Storage units are a racket

Have you ever stopped to notice the number of sprawling storage units in your area? They seem to have popped up everywhere, and for good reason. There's a booming business in banking on people not being able to let go of their useless shit.

We are so reluctant to clear the clutter that we will pay someone hundreds, if not thousands, of dollars a year to store it out of our sight. We intend to have our cake and eat it, too. That's the American way!

Don't get me wrong, there are plenty of legitimate reasons to rent a storage unit. Maybe a family member passed and you needed to clear out the house quickly. Or maybe you're transitioning to a new home that isn't quite ready yet. But if, like most people, you're using a storage unit like a very detached garage, it's time to get your shit together.

Seriously, what are you doing to yourself? Entire TV shows are based around the rarity of finding useful or valuable objects in a storage unit. **If you're willing to store something several miles away from you, I'm willing to bet you don't fucking need it in your life.**

Do me a favor. Imagine, for a moment, throwing open the gate to your storage unit and selling every single thing in it to a pack of strangers. Does that bum you out?* If not,

---

*Here's a little bonus tip: If you get excited about the thought of making money off of something, you don't like it enough to keep it. The things that make you happy are priceless.

I repeat: What are you doing to yourself? You're forking over your hard-earned cash every month to hold on to things you don't actually want.

Enough. There is no earthly reason for you to rent a storage unit. Once you build up your "fuck it" muscles, I want you to tackle that overly secure dumpster. Does anything in it make you happy? If yes, move those items to your house—where you put the shit you actually care about. If no, into the donate pile it goes. By the end of the day, you had better be turning in your key and cancelling your lease.

....

Your Chapter 2 Checklist

* Do one quick sweep of the house and pull out anything that pisses you off
* Build up your "fuck it" muscles by starting with the easy stuff
* Picture your happy place and get rid of shit that doesn't fit the bill
* Keep what makes you *happy*, not just meh
* Measure everything against something you really love

* Upgrade the practical crap to alternatives that make you smile
* Help yourself focus by picking a project and racing the clock
* Save the family heirlooms for after your "fuck it" muscles come in
* Tell friends and family to mind their own damn business while you work
* Worry 'bout yourself and leave other people's crap alone
* Donate your shit to charity, not to unwitting family members who don't need it
* Do not Netflix and tidy
* Decide once and don't second-guess yourself
* Treat gifts like any other item in the house: love it or lose it
* Don't be the asshole who pays money to store useless crap

3

How to Organize Your Sh*t

Getting down to brass tacks

I know what you're thinking. *OK, I get it. Everything in my home should make me happy. Awesome. But where the fuck do I even start?* **You start with whatever feels easiest right this minute.** (If you're like me, clothing probably isn't anywhere near the top of that list.)

What are you least attached to? Let's say it's your shoes. So you go around the house and gather up every sneaker, high heel, and snow boot you can find. Dump them all on a large surface, like your living room floor (if you can find it). First, pull out the ones you can't live without because you love them so much. Theoretically those should be the only keepers, but let's get real. People like options.

Next, separate out the obvious tosses—shoes that are worn out, disgusting, uncomfortable, or that you bought for that wedding five years ago. Don't start in with the buts—you are never going to wear these shoes again. Keeping old shoes around just to look at them is weird. Be better than that.

Now look at the leftovers and check for overlap. How many fucking pairs of Old Navy flip-flops could you possibly need? I guarantee you're not wearing all seventeen pairs. You probably wear three of them regularly, so throw those three pairs with the keepers and toss the rest into the "to-go" pile. (If wearing an endless array of colorful plastic footwear makes you happy, ignore this paragraph.)

Keep thinking about your goal: to keep only the things that make you happy, that you use, and that fit into the life you want for yourself. Remember when you thought you wanted to take up hiking, so you bought those really expensive hiking boots and then didn't set foot on a fucking trail? Embrace the fact that you like yoga, indoors, where it's temperature controlled and you have ready access to cucumber water, and then sell those bad boys on eBay.

If you're overly attached to your shoes, start with something else. You get the idea. You have to learn to be decisive and hold yourself accountable—two things most people aren't super awesome at. The more you practice that with the little things, the easier it'll be when you get to the big things. (You're also going to break things down into doable subsections to keep yourself from running screaming from the house, Wile E. Coyote style.)

I'm starting with books, but if your personal collection rivals the town library, maybe you leave that one for later. Work on building up those "fuck it" muscles with something small that you don't really care about but have been meaning to tackle—whatever that is for you. If you follow my road map, you'll have your shit together in no time! (No promises, though. I don't know how far gone you are.)

Books

It's not a fucking trophy case

OK, so this one is controversial. The idea of getting rid of your books may spark more outrage than joy, especially if you're a self-proclaimed bibliophile. But with no folding or special storage requirements, I still think books are a good place to start.

Bookshelves tend to be weighed down by everything a person's ever read plus the books they think they *should* read. **A book collection isn't a résumé—it's a love letter.** We get it, you read *War and Peace*. Good for you. Unless you loved it beyond reason, stop being a pretentious jackass and pass it on to someone who hasn't read it.

Now that millennials and Marvel movies have made nerds cool (not complaining), people are even more precious about their book collections. I love books. You would definitely call me a book lover. But my book collection is not for show. And yours shouldn't be either.

Toss all the books you own into a pile on the floor and get to work. Sort them first into Read and Unread. **The most important thing to remember while you're clearing things out is NOT to start reading the books.** Now is not the time to leaf through the pages of *Yes Please* and relive the magic that is Amy Poehler. Now is the time to judge a book by its cover.

Of the books you've read, pull out the ones you want to be buried with. Those are the keepers. (Yes, it's an intentionally high bar.) Make another little pile of books you love and want others to love. Those go to new homes. Of the books you haven't read, pick out the ones you'd buy if you were in a bookstore right now. Those go on a special shelf. (More on that later.)

Everything that's left? They all go in the donation bin. Breathe. It's OK. It will not kill you to unload books you've already read/will never read/don't even like that much. I promise. From now on, you're going to have higher standards for what makes it onto your bookshelves.

You're always going to want to put great reads in that place of honor, but don't turn up your nose at the alternatives. If you want a quick beach read, grab it from the library. If you want to go back to a favorite again and again, Kindle really can't be beat. (That tightness in your

chest at the mention of e-readers is the old you—the you
that treated your book collection like a trophy case.
Breathe through the self-importance.)

Get real—you're never reading that

Take a good, hard look at your pile of unread books. You
had always planned on reading them someday, when you
had the time/energy/brain cells. But you always found
something else to read, didn't you? Someday will never
come for most of those poor little guys.

Now you need to be honest about the ones you genuinely
want to read. (Not the ones you think you *should* read.)
Look at each book, read the back, and decide if you would
buy that book for list price right now. If not, it goes in the
Donate pile. Don't think about the fact that you bought it
for three dollars at a yard sale. If you aren't willing to pay
list price, you don't really want that book. You just wanted
the bargain.

Worst case scenario, you decide you want to read
something you've chucked, so you take your lazy ass to the
library and check it out. The library's great, because it
gives you a time limit. You finish that fucker in three weeks
or you don't finish it at all. OK, yes, you can probably
renew it . . . several times. But if you challenge yourself to

finish it quickly, you're less likely to lose interest in the story and more likely to get to the other books on your list.

I'm going to tell you the secret no bibliophile wants you to know: you don't have to finish a book you don't like. If it's sitting in your unread pile because you stopped caring two chapters in, get rid of the damn thing. Sure, there are a few books I've had to start twice before realizing how amazing they are. But if you feel you've really given it a chance, there's no shame in quitting. There's only shame in living like a hoarder because you adhere to useless unwritten rules about reading.

The next time you start to get click-happy on Amazon, remember all of those sad, unread books taking up space and collecting dust on your bookshelves. Instead of instinctively hitting "Place your order," click on "Add to wishlist" instead. If you're still desperate to read the book a few months down the road: library. (If you thought I was going to say buy it, you haven't been paying attention.)

As for the handful of books in your Unread pile that you genuinely want to read, they get their own special place in your home. Store them close to where you like to read, in plain sight. Then make a plan to actually read them. Even committing to just fifteen minutes a day is better than nothing.

Proudly display your "desert island" picks

If you love a book, let it go. If it doesn't come back to you . . . well, that was pretty fucking predictable. People really suck at returning books. Am I the only one with a list of friends who aren't allowed to borrow books anymore? If they stop speaking to you, there goes your original copy of *Wicked*. Now all you can get is the musical tie-in edition with the stupid black-and-green cover.

Yes, of course you should be generous with your books. The ideas and worlds they comprise are meant to be shared. But you're not an asshole if you hold on to a few more tightly than others. You're only an asshole if you don't return an original copy of *Wicked* to its rightful owner, who fell in love with it long before Broadway did. (At this point, I would rather use my hard-earned money to buy someone a copy of my favorite book than loan my copy to them.)

Your book collection is just for you. Looking at it should make you feel *happy*, not accomplished. If you're letting books collect dust on overcrowded shelves so you can pat yourself on the back for being well read, see my previous note about not being a pretentious jackass.

The books you love most in this world should get a prized place in your home. Give them room to shine on spacious shelves. Display them facing out, or in little groupings with picture frames and flower vases like you're one of the Property Brothers.

These coveted few should be the only books on your shelves because you've donated or loaned everything else. You can love a book and it still does not make the "desert island" cut. Pass it on to someone else who will love it just as much. Tell them to keep it moving. Don't have anyone in your life who can appreciate it? Book bins and Little Free Libraries are popping up everywhere and making it easy to keep the story going.

So what happens if a book makes your "desert island" cut but you followed my earlier advice and checked it out of the library? You buy it. See how easy that is? You would have bought it anyway, but now you know it's a good purchase. More often than not, though, you'll be quite happy to give a book back to the library at the end of three weeks and you'll have saved yourself twenty bucks and some shelf space.

Magazines get a special shout-out

For some of you, magazines are your books. Whether you subscribe to *BH&G* or pick up gossip rags at the checkout counter, those babies can pile up fast. Maybe you bought one but didn't have time to read it yet. Or there was an article in one that you want to take a closer look at (when you're not distracted by *NCIS*). Or there's a product in one that you want to remember.

But when it comes time to remember that product, you have to dig through a couple dozen magazines to find it. Which one has the website for the beard wax you want to buy Mark for Christmas? All you can remember is that it had a picture of a pumpkin on the cover. That narrows it down to eight, because the lead-up to Thanksgiving lasts from July to October in Marketing Land. (Fun system we have now, right? The one where you can find Halloween candy and Christmas candy in the same aisle? Really helps you live in the moment. And keep your weight down.)

How about this? Read the damn thing when you get it, rip out the shit you want, and get rid of the rest.* That's not so hard, right? If you have a tower of magazines that's ready to topple, toss them all now and start fresh. Throw them in the recycle bin or pass them along to someone else. (You can always find someone who's too cheap to

---

*Catalogs: Second verse, same as the first. Keep the coupons, recycle the rest. Actually, don't even keep the coupons. You don't need the temptation.

subscribe.) Then maybe think about cancelling some of those subscriptions.

Papers

Your smartphone is your BFF

So much of our lives are digital these days. We let tiny robots give us weather reports, we call taxis through an app, we even hang out with friends and family via video chat. So why wouldn't we use tech to help us get our shit together? **If you have a smartphone, you have everything you need to conquer your paper clutter in the palm of your hand.**

First, stem the tide of papers that comes into your home. Whip out that smartphone and change as many bills and statements as you can to their paperless counterparts (check out page 67 for more on that). Then head to the websites of any magazines or catalogs you get but don't read and cancel your subscriptions. In just a few minutes, your smartphone has already helped you keep clutter from taking over your dining room table. (Be honest—that table is just a way station for random crap. You eat in front of the TV.)

Unfortunately, paperless statements alone won't help you escape the constant barrage of useless crap that ends up in your mailbox. If you ever want to see your table again, you need to go through and get rid of as many of those papers as possible. Recycle what you can, shred what you need to,* and you should be left with just the actionable stuff and important documents.

If you're keeping something as a reminder, put it on your to-do list (or tell Alexa to remind you) and toss the paper. Move important legal documents to a fire-proof sleeve or safe. If you come across greeting cards, photos, or other sentimental items, set them aside for later. In fact, don't even look at them. You're not ready. You don't have your "fuck it" muscles yet.

For any papers that aren't covered in this section, I'll just remind you that a little common sense goes a long way. I used to tear the return addresses off Christmas card envelopes because I can't keep a street address in my head. (When you need to send a sympathy card, you really don't want to ask for the recipient's address.) After searching for

---

*If you don't have a shredder, you still have options for disposing of sensitive papers. Some towns offer a free shredding event (usually after tax time), and you can find plenty of places nearby that offer shredding services for a small fee.

those tiny strips of paper a few times, I realized how fucking stupid my system was and took the two minutes to enter the addresses into my phone's contacts. Now they're forever backed up to the cloud and easily accessible whenever I need them. Work smarter, not harder, people.

Get your inspiration from better sources

Do you have a file full of recipes and DIY articles that you've torn out? Have you ever actually made anything from them? Of course not, because the closest you come to cooking is watching Gordon Ramsay scare the crap out of mediocre chefs.

I'm all for hanging on to what inspires you, but what good is it doing if you don't look at it? If you haven't done anything with that folder, it's time to toss it. But if there's anything in that folder that actually makes you happy just to see it, hang it up somewhere. Frame a bunch of tear-outs and make a gallery wall. (You may not know how to make origami napkin rings, but they're so pretty to look at! Don't worry about what other people will think—it's your fucking wall.)

Can't live without your inspo file? Digitize it. Pinterest was literally made for this, but you could also use a note-taking app like Google Keep or Evernote. Keep that paint color handy by snapping a pic and uploading it. Google that delicious-looking orange chicken and pin the recipe you like best (for someone else to cook *for* you, obviously). Not only will you find an endless array to choose from, you'll also get to see comments and reviews from people who have actually tried them. A ripped piece of paper can't give you that.

Reclaim the refrigerator

If you have kids in your life, your refrigerator probably looks like a Jackson Pollock painting. By all means, keep it the way it is if you smile every time you look at it. But don't feel guilty about paring down if it drives you crazy. It's your fridge, in your kitchen, and it shouldn't give you anxiety every time you walk past it.

Instead, use the fridge as a place of honor for one, maybe two pieces of your kid's artwork. As for the rest, take pictures and (covertly) recycle the originals. Eventually, you can choose your favorites and make a sleek little photo book. Kids are tiny narcissists—they'll love having their artwork immortalized in print and you'll avoid a bin overflowing with old finger paintings.

It's the 21st century: time for paperless statements

If you still receive paper statements of any kind, just know that I am rolling my eyes at you. Normally, I wouldn't judge. But come on. There is absolutely no fucking reason for you to receive a paper copy of a credit card statement. You can search years' worth of transactions online, get custom spending alerts sent to your phone, and see your credit score in a free app.

Don't trust yourself to check your email? Sign up for text alerts. You can also set up automatic bill payments in your checking account. It's free and easy. (If it's not free, it's time to switch banks, because fees are bullshit.)

Don't trust your bank not to get hacked? When did you become your Grandma June, hiding money under your mattress because you can't trust "the man"? Get over it. Credit card companies, service providers, and banks have some of the best encryption in the biz.* How secure do you think your recycle bin is when you put it at the curb with all your mail in it?

---

*That's not an excuse to be a dumbass. Your bank can't protect you if you leave your unlocked phone at the mall and all of your passwords are saved.

Take a minute right now to log in to all of your accounts and switch to paperless statements. Seriously. Put the book down, download the apps or pull up the websites, log on, and sign up. Not only will you make your life easier, you'll also be helping to chip away at the endless stream of garbage that ends up in our landfills and oceans. That's one hell of a win-win.

Speaking of which, please don't be the asshole who prints out payment confirmations, tax documents, contracts, and other shit you can access with the click of a button or store in a Google drive. Ink is too fucking expensive to waste on hard copies you don't even need and that will end up in the trash to be rifled through by petty thieves.

Have stereo instructions ever been useful?

We all have that stack of papers that came with crap we bought. You've got the warranty for your toaster oven, instructions for putting together your IKEA dresser, the manual that came with your fancy DSLR, and about a dozen other unnecessary documents. Not only are these things basically illegible, they're redundant, thanks to the Internet. You can safely recycle everything in that pile.

Do I feel you hesitating? Think about it. Did you register the toaster oven? Probably not, so the warranty papers are useless. Are you ever going to dismantle the dresser that took you three hours to build? Hell no. Don't know how to use your sewing machine? Guess what! Thousands of people on the Internet do.

Ninety-nine times out of a hundred, you're never even going to crack open any of these documents. For that last one percent, you'll find everything you need online. Most manuals can be found right on the manufacturers' websites. But when you need help with something, you know you're just going to watch a YouTube video of someone showing you how to do it. Embrace the easy.

If you didn't learn it the first time . . .

Study materials from continuing education—or worse, primary education—just need to go. Be honest with yourself. You're never going to look at them again. Deep down you know that if it didn't stick the first time, it's not worth worrying about a second time. Just accept where you are and toss the lot. (And if there's something you need to know down the road, there's this handy thing called *Google*. Check it out sometime.)

If you're a current student, keep only the notes and materials for the classes you're actively taking. (That means you get to do a cathartic purge at the end of every semester!) And keep in mind that you're probably only going to have this one shot at learning what's in them. You think you don't need the GenEds, but what you learn there will save your ass when you have to make small talk at office parties ten years from now.*

Don't leave the money stuff lying around

If any of your papers involve money, they need to be shredded. Having paychecks, deposit slips, used checkbook registers, tax documents, or credit card statements hanging around the place is just asking for identity theft. Someone breaks into your house and gets not only your TV but also your social security number? That's a really bad night. And it can be prevented by not saving any of that stuff in the first place.

Go paperless, stop printing shit out, and this shouldn't be a problem. Plus, you'll find it a hell of a lot easier to

---

*Speaking of the office, if you have the option of using direct deposit and you don't use it because you don't trust money that doesn't touch your hands, we can't be friends. Area 51 is just a military base, the Loch Ness Monster was a big fish spotted by a drunken boater, and you cannot break your mother's back if you step on a crack. Get your shit together. Direct deposit saves you time, anxiety, and clutter. (Ghosts are totally real, though.)

open an app than to thumb through a filing cabinet. Save that level of paper organization for the office, where they're scared of all things new and digital.

If you really can't bring yourself to go totally paperless, at least shred anything older than a month. And maybe preempt any problems by using one of those info-guarding stamps on all the sensitive stuff as soon as something comes in.

When you're done tidying up, your financial papers shouldn't take up a whole filing cabinet. In fact, you shouldn't even have a filing cabinet. It means you're wasting too much space with unnecessary crap. At most, you should have one file folder of important documents (in a fireproof bag) and one folder of things that can be recycled or shredded when you're finished with them.

Random crap

If it doesn't have a home, its home is in the trash

We all have a junk drawer . . . or a junk bin. OK, maybe you're like Monica Geller and have a Closet of Shame that hides your mess. Honestly, you're always going to have at least a little pile of random crap that you don't really need but can't give up. Spare key rings, buttons, maybe the odd McDonald's toy—it all ends up together on the Island of Misfit Crap. Getting to physical Inbox Zero is a pipe dream, so just aim for minimizing the damage.

First, remove anything that actually has a home to which you were too damn lazy to return it, and put it all away. You might be surprised by how much of your junk drawer you clear out just doing this. **Then, check whatever's left against the gold standard: Do you like it and/or do you use it?**

Keep in mind that "But I might need it someday" is still not a fucking option. How many times have you actually needed something that falls into the "I might need it" category? Those items definitely go in the donation pile or the garbage. (I'm looking at you, buttons.) And if something is broken, don't kid yourself—your lazy ass is not going to fix it. Garbage.

Whatever's left should have passed the happy test. (Are those buttons I see? I'll wait.) Now you need to spend a little time finding that random-but-useful crap a proper home. For example, you use batteries, but only if you can find them and they work. Gather up all the batteries you have and test those you're not sure about.*

Once you have a stockpile of perfectly functional batteries, you have to designate a logical place for them. Where is up to you, but make sure you're going to remember they're there when you need them. (Personally, I wouldn't put them in with the toothpaste. But if you use a battery-powered toothbrush, maybe that makes the most sense to you.) Bonus points if you use rechargeable batteries and store the charger with them.

Go through this same process with whatever useful things have ended up in your Closet of Shame. You'll feel so much better when you have a tidy drawer or an empty "I'll deal with this later" bin and everything you need is neatly put away. Then you can move on to all the other places random crap tends to accumulate.

---

*You can buy a cheap tester online or at the big box stores. Believe me, it's less annoying than putting twenty dead batteries, one by one, into your TV remote and finding out none of them work. And for fuck's sake, stop throwing dead batteries in drawers! Throw them in the trash where they belong, and then you can add the tester to the donate pile for some other lazy asshole to use.

Your kitchen is full of random crap

It's easy for unnecessary crap to accumulate in your kitchen. You probably have more storage there than anywhere else in the house, and kitchen gadgets are too fun to pass up. Do you really need that cherry pitter? Probably not. But if the guillotine action of that bright red utensil makes you happy, why not keep it? You can find plenty of other places to cut back. (You may also want to look into some yoga or meditation for your anger issues. Just saying.)

Let's say you have eight spatulas of varying sizes and shapes. You probably reach for only two of them regularly, so the rest can go in the donation pile. (If you're wondering if you can *like* a spatula, you clearly haven't used a polka-dotted spoonula that says "Lick Me.") And what fucking good are food storage containers without lids? Recycle bin. When's the last time you used the immersion blender? Donation pile. And that's just the tip of the iceberg.

The kitchen is an easy place to get carried away with your aspirations—especially after a few episodes of *The Great British Baking Show*. When you bought that roasting pan, you were sure you were going to use it constantly. But it turns out that you're lazy and hate to cook, so maybe you embrace the takeout and get rid of the gadgets. You can give it a few months to see if your culinary talents emerge, but then it's time to pare down. The same goes for uneaten food and ingredients. You had the best of intentions when you bought the makings for macarons. But half of them have expired and you still don't have a jar full of delightful French confections. Go through your cupboards and get real about what you will and won't use, and what's too late to try. Toss everything that's open or expired, and donate the rest to your local food pantry.

How many fucking pens do you need?

Are you a pen hoarder? Do you go crazy when faced with colorful stationery and notebooks?

Do you get carried away in office supply stores? Before you know it, notecards and paperclips have taken over your guest bedroom. (That's where you put the little desk you never use, because you do your work at work like a normal person who doesn't get paid enough to care outside of business hours.)

Start with the pens. Clearly, you don't need as many as you have. As a pen hoarder myself, I'll allow a few more pens than might be strictly reasonable, but don't go crazy.

Keep the ones that make you happy when you see them or use them, whether that's a fancy monogrammed Parker or the Bic you stole from a motel. Then go through the usual selection process for the rest of your office clutter. Once you've rooted out all of the excess, give it to a school or library that could use the supplies.

Again, be honest about what you actually need. More than any other category of random crap, office supplies are meant to be used, not admired. It's OK to keep a stationery set you love, but stockpiling stationery when you don't write letters is just dumb. Get a pen pal or give the stationery to someone who'll actually use it.

Your bathroom should not look like an Ulta Beauty

We all have our weaknesses, and free samples are definitely one of mine. How great is it to get to try something new before you buy it? If you don't like it, you've saved (sometimes significant amounts of) money and product. No downside, right?

Wrong. Now you have dozens of tiny tubes, cards, bottles, and sprays cluttering up your bathroom cabinet because you can't finish them all and you don't want to throw something away unused. Which is why you also have several half-empty regular-size bottles of shampoo, conditioner, and body wash.

For this one, you need to do a big purge. Put all of your makeup, skincare, and beauty products in one place so that you can see the breadth of your addiction. Snap a mental picture (or a real one) and pull it up before you step foot in Sephora again. If you've stopped using something because you found something better, out it goes. If you bought the real product because you loved the sample, add the sample to your travel stuff.

If you didn't love something, trash it and embrace the guilt—it may just keep you from impulse-buying the next new thing. Of course, you can mitigate some of the guilt by passing good products along to family and friends who you know would like to try them. If you work in a big office with people you like, you could also leave the products in the bathroom with a "free to good home" sign. (You'd be surprised how fast they go!)

Whatever you do with all your excess products, just get them out of your home. Then maybe cancel a few of your beauty subscriptions and find a twelve-step program to deal with your FOMO and susceptibility to marketing. (When you do, let me know where to meet up.)

No, you don't need an Ethernet cable

Let me guess: somewhere in your house, you have a bin full of cables, cords, chargers, adapters, old phones, an old Nintendo DS, and a flashlight? Maybe you keep your lightbulbs in there, too. And you can't tell one thing from another because it's a tangled mess.

First, deal with everything that's not a cord: Give the lightbulbs their own designated place before you break them. Put the flashlight in your nightstand so you have easy access if you need it. (Make sure it has working batteries.) Reset and donate the old phones and their chargers to charity. And find a new home for that DS you haven't used in five years—somewhere there's a six-year-old girl or a 22-year-old guy who would love to have it.

Finally, tackle the snake pit. We tend to hold on to every cord that crosses our paths because we might need it. But if you've been keeping up, you know that "I might need it" is a bullshit excuse to hoard unnecessary crap. So if it doesn't plug into something you own, it goes. If it plugs into something you don't use, they both go.

Pair up the adapters with their appliances and keep matching sets together from now on. Any adapters that are left over are probably from something you threw away years ago, so you clearly don't need them. Toss the Ethernet cable you've had since 1998 and any TV cables you're holding on to—your TV is already hooked up and cables are cheap if you need them.

Finally, go through your chargers and ditch any that are frayed or don't work with your current phone. Put a current one everywhere you might need one (desk, car, purse, nightstand). If you have any leftovers, keep ONE spare and donate the rest. There's no fucking excuse for "I might need it" here. You can buy a new one pretty much anywhere but the Taco Bell drive-thru (for now).

Ditch the DVDs (and Blu-Rays)

How often do you really watch movies on disc? I mean, when was the last time you actually thought *I want to watch* Forgetting Sarah Marshall *right now* and made the effort to take the movie out of its case, put it in the DVD player, switch your TV's input to DVD, and watch it? That's what I thought.

Nope, we are officially too fucking lazy for DVDs. More often than not, you come across movies on TV and deal with the commercials because it's easy, right? Or you find something to stream instead. So ditch the DVDs and reclaim your shelf space. You can sell them for a dollar at a yard sale and put the money toward digital copies of your favorites. (Or just donate them to a local thrift store because you're too busy to have a yard sale.)

If you really can't part with your DVD collection, at least toss the cases. You can recycle the plastic and put all of your movies in a CD/DVD binder with clear sleeves. Suddenly your entire movie collection takes up three inches of shelving instead of the whole bookcase. If you're really persnickety, you can even find ones that have sleeves for the covers, which easily slip out of the cases. But trust me, that's more work than it's worth.

The American version of a savings account (the piggybank)

People who leave loose change all over the house aggravate the crap out of me. That's actual money. Maybe it means less to Americans because we don't have any large-denomination coins. But all that loose change adds up to dollar bills, people.

Buy yourself a piggy bank (a cute one that makes you happy) and start filling it up. When it's stuffed, don't start leaving your fucking money in random places again. Take Ms. Piggy to the bank or your local coin-sorting machine and turn your coins into real cash. Then treat yourself to a nice dinner with the proceeds. You'd be surprised at how much that little bank holds.

Honorable mention: empty boxes

Do you have a stockpile of empty boxes from purchases you might need to store or return? Because packing them in the boxes is neater than storing them without? Well, do you know what's not neat? Keeping all of your clothes in a laundry basket on the floor because your closet is full of useless empty boxes. If you absolutely must, break them down and keep them banded together in the attic or garage. But once you decide you're keeping something (you have 14 days—I don't care what your damn receipt says), it's time to recycle the box.

And if you hoard delivery boxes around the holidays, just stop. It's not worth the ugly tower of cardboard for the one box you're actually going to end up using. Go to the dollar store and buy a two-pack of gift boxes like a normal person. Or make life easy on yourself and get the two-pack of gift bags instead. (Seriously, you can't go wrong with gift wrap from the dollar store.)

Clothing

You have too many fucking sweaters

If you piled all of the clothing you have into a heap on your bed, you'd probably be fucking mortified at the sight. One person could not possibly need all of that clothing. How on earth did you end up with so many sweaters? You have fifty-three pairs of socks? You still have that blazer from your first job interview? This is a problem.

Let's settle one thing right now: you're not going to whittle this mountain down to a capsule wardrobe in one go. You didn't go on a crazy rich-kid shopping spree and buy all of this at once. (If you did, call me. I'll be your shopping buddy next time.) You picked it up a little at a time. And you're going to have to work on getting rid of it a little at a time. Unless you drastically change your shopping habits, you'll probably have to work on it for the rest of your life. (Just reading that makes you want to drastically change your shopping habits, right?)

So where do you even start? Odds are, you've been wearing the clothes you like best. Try this little experiment: For a couple of weeks, put everything you wear and wash into a different drawer, or even a laundry basket. If you have to dig through the basket for something you want to wear, it's a good indication that it's a keeper. Most of the things in the basket probably are. The ones you should worry about are those that didn't make it into the basket. Go through your closet and drawers and ask yourself why you haven't been reaching for what's there.

Unpulled tags and sealed packages are a red flag. You haven't liked it or used it, so don't think twice before donating or selling it. **Clothing is meant to be worn, not just looked at longingly as you reach past it for your go-to outfits.** If you're waiting for the right occasion to wear that dress, create one. Wear it to the grocery store—who gives a fuck? Stop waiting for somedays that might never come.

When you're ready to start discarding, take out a few things that you absolutely love to wear. They could be a pair of funny socks, a work top that makes you feel like a boss, and a flirty summer dress—as long as they make you happier than you can logically explain. Compare all of the things you haven't been wearing to these favorites. Do they even come close? If they don't make you even a little giddy when you think about wearing them, you *won't* wear them. Time for those pieces to meet their new owners.

We've established that donating items can help take the sting out of letting them go, and that's especially true with clothing. Too many people in this country go without the clothing they need, so you can feel good about giving away that coat you never wore. But don't use donation as a crutch to assuage your guilt. No one wants that threadbare cardigan with the hole in it, and if you donate it, the charity is just going to have to waste their resources throwing it out. You bought fast fashion. You can't be bothered to sew the hole. Deal with your guilt, throw the damn thing out, and make better choices next time.

You may come across a piece that doesn't necessarily make you happy but that you find useful, like a thermal tank you wear under sweaters in the winter. As long as you actually use it, it meets the keeper criteria. But check out "The practical approach to joy" on page 30 and consider swapping that boring tank for a comfy camisole in a color or pattern that makes you smile.

If you're still having trouble deciding what stays and what goes, go shopping. (No, not literally. Have you learned nothing?) Pretend your bedroom is a store and everything is $40. Go through every piece of clothing you have and ask yourself: Would I pay $40 for this right now? If you don't like it enough to spend $40 on it, you don't like it enough to keep it. Out it goes. This trick really puts into perspective the things you only bought because they were on sale.

Remember, the point of this whole book is to find a way to surround yourself with things that make you happy. **Imagine opening your closet door and seeing only clothes you love.** Putting an outfit together in the morning goes from being a chore to being a joy because you get to wear things that make you feel good. That's the goal. Keep it in mind when you're hemming and hawing over a shirt you don't like but feel guilty about ditching.

You're entitled to your sweatpants

If you have more pajama bottoms than any other piece of clothing, I feel you. I can't turn down a pair of cute and comfy PJ pants. And as long as I'm wearing everything in that drawer on a regular basis, I'm not about to feel bad about it.

Not only do I not care about feeling "elegant" when I'm on the couch watching reruns of *Psych*, I am also not here for hand-washing silky nightgowns. I want my laundry to be quick and painless, so I buy things that I can throw in the washer without worrying. But that's me. If silky nightgowns make you happy, channel your inner Blanche Devereaux and go to town.

The same goes for loungewear and athleisure. Maybe you've never done a sun salutation in your life, but you slip into yoga pants the second you come home from work. Or maybe you like to keep your power suit on right up until you head for bed. Who cares? Are you comfortable? Are you happy? Cool. Wear whatever the fuck you want to.

A messy heap takes up more space than tidy items

Most of us are so lazy that we do a half-assed job of folding the laundry and then haphazardly shove the items into drawers so full we can barely close them. How does that work for you when you need to get dressed in the morning? How much easier would life be if you didn't have so many fucking things to fold and put away?

That's why it's important to narrow down your clothing collection first. When you're done discarding, the content of your drawers should be loose enough that you can easily see and reach everything in them. Take things a step further by neatly folding everything before storing it, and you'll never again have to toss a drawer like a burglar who just heard a car pull up.

If you can't see it, you won't wear it

The great thing about getting rid of the shit you don't like is that you're guaranteed to be happy with whatever you pull out of your drawers. But if you still have a good amount of stuff after culling, you'll need to organize it well. You're not going to remember what you have unless you can see it. (Oh, you have a photographic memory? Yay for you, Lexipedia, but you're not exempt.)

The best solution is a big closet with a mixture of shelves and rods. Clothing that's hung up and folded neatly on shelves at eye level (instead of in overcrowded drawers) is more likely to be seen and worn. But we don't always get to choose the storage space we have. Make the best of what you've got just by giving your clothing a little breathing room.

Hang up dresses, suits, and anything that you wouldn't want to throw in the dryer to de-wrinkle before wearing it. One-size-fits-all is just as fucking ridiculous in organizing as it is in clothing, so when it comes to arranging your closet, do whatever your little heart desires. Hang things by color, by material, by use—hell, hang them by button size, if that's what makes sense to you. Just make sure there's enough space between each hanger to really see what you have.

Some items really shouldn't be hung, like knit sweaters that "grow" if left too long on hangers. (When you finally put one on, you'll have weird shit going on at your shoulders because the hanger has stretched out the fabric there.) Choosing a different kind of hanger isn't going to help. Some things you just have to fold, which naturally makes them harder to see.

It doesn't matter how you fold things as long as you can easily leaf through them to find what you need. Again, space is key—shove everything into an overflowing drawer and you're bound to lose a few items at the bottom of the heap. If you go the traditional route and lay clothes on top of each other, make sure it's a shallow stack. If you use the rolling method (famous for saving room in your suitcase), aim for one layer per drawer. And if you still can't fit everything into your storage space, you haven't gotten rid of enough crap. Try again.

It's a closet, not an Oreo—don't overstuff it

Most of us store a hell of a lot more than clothes in our closets. Maybe you're disciplined and only store clothing-adjacent items like shoes, handbags, and accessories. Or maybe you're like me and store everything from Christmas gifts to cat toys* in there. But if you hope to use any of what you have in there, you have to go through the same old steps: pare down, put back what makes you happy, and leave some space around all of it. If you don't have enough space for clothing, accessories, cat toys, *and* breathing room, you'll need to find new storage solutions for a few things.

Life is too fucking short to fold your underwear

This may go against conventional organizing wisdom, but I don't really give a damn if your underwear drawer looks like Day 5 at the Victoria's Secret Semi-Annual Sale. Throw them all in a drawer and be done with it. As long as you've purged the ones you don't like, you should be able to blindly reach a hand in and pull out something suitable.

Socks are another story. On top of your general mood, you'll be choosing your socks based on what shoes you're wearing, what the weather's like, and who knows what

---

*You have to cycle your cat toys. Otherwise, cats get bored and you end up buying expensive things with electronic mice in a desperate attempt to appease the cat that won't stop scratching your carpet. Spoiler alert: he'd be happier with a tennis ball.

other criteria. Get rid of anything with a hole (your lazy ass is not going to sew the hole), anything that's threadbare, and anything you just don't like. Keep the ones you actually enjoy wearing, and organize them however you like.

I personally love silly socks. Most of the time, no one but you is going to see them, so they become a little inside joke if they're colorful or carry an off-color message. Because crazy socks make me happy, I allow myself a number of them that borders on absurd. If socks are just socks to you, then all you need is the bare minimum—enough to get you to laundry day.

Of course, the point is to be able to easily grab what you want when you want it. If you have to dig through layers of socks to find your favorites (the ones that say "Fuck off, I'm reading"), you have too many socks or you've stored them in too small a space. I'm going to trust you to use your brain and figure out which problem you have and how to fix it.

If you're worried about stretching out your socks and stockings, fold or roll them instead of balling them up the way Mom taught you. (How should you fold your socks, you ask? They're socks, not puff pastry. Just fold the damn things.)

Finally, be mindful when shopping for new socks. Stop buying them in bulk in sad, plastic packages. That's not going to make anyone happy. How fucking hard is it to buy a pair of socks when you need one? Treat yourself to some covered in unicorn kittens that make you giggle when you slip them on.

Where to put your parka in June

Unless you're Mrs. Howell (pre-Island getaway), you probably don't swap out clothing based on the change of season. More likely, you have a few truly seasonal items amid a lot of layering pieces. That means you can tackle tidying up your clothing whenever you feel like it rather than working on it four times a year.

Sundresses and lightweight scarves are probably already in the mix, but don't forget to break out those bathing suits and ear muffs while you're in the mood to throw shit out. (It's too easy to buy a new pair of fluffy mittens before you bother to haul out your winter gear and find you already own some.) All of the seasonal stuff gets held to the same standard: Do you like it and do you use it? That includes beach towels, cover-ups, sun hats, mittens, scarves, beanies, long underwear, and heavy winter coats. If you're one person, you don't need more than six beach towels. (You're starting to catch on, right? Yeah, two's the max.)

The goal is to pare down your clothing enough to accommodate all seasons in your day-to-day stock. But if you just can't squeeze it all in, you can tuck the summer and winter stuff away separately. These are the items you only use when it's genuinely hot or cold out (not to be confused with the light jacket you think is seasonal but actually use three seasons out of the year). Cordoning off just the extremes gives you more space without sacrificing convenience.

Do yourself a favor and don't store this stuff in plastic tubs. That fossil-fuel smell takes forever to wash out. Breathable fabric bins stored under a bed or on a top closet shelf are your best bet. It goes without saying, but the more you discard, the less space you'll have to give up for bins of excess crap.

Memory Lane

Carve out a day for this one

You made it to the end of your discarding journey! Hopefully, by now your "fuck it" muscles are nice and strong, you've become a decision-making ninja, and you're excited about your happy place taking shape. Keep that motivation handy, because you'll need it for this part.

Take a moment to think about what you want to accomplish before you start in. People think Memory Lane is like Mayberry, but when it comes to tidying, it's more like that miniature town in *Big Fish* that no one's allowed to leave. If you're not careful, you could get sucked in and lose all track of time and space.

When it comes to sorting through keepsakes, you just have to ask yourself one question: Does it make you happy? Old report cards are kind of cool to see, but you can't say that they make you happy. The same goes for childhood trophies and awards. And your parents would probably appreciate your old art-class doodles, but even they won't want to keep them.

Of course, if you're just not ready to part with some things, you can find ways to compromise. You don't want to be a grown-ass adult with a Beanie Baby collection, but you can certainly hang on to a couple of your favorites. (Just check eBay before you donate those guys—find the right crazy person, and Claude the Crab could buy your ticket to Maui.)

You'll need to remind yourself that it's the memory that

makes you happy, not the thing. If you're really honest with yourself, not much of your "memory bin" meets the keeper criteria. And unless you own something that's meant to be passed down or that will appreciate for real money (we're talking jewels, not Beanie Babies), there's just no point in keeping it. **Your kids don't want to have to deal with your grade-school crap after you're gone.**

Resistance is futile

Storing untouched bins of old baseball cards and half-finished photo albums isn't the only way we resist dealing with our keepsakes. Sometimes we send them back where they came from—our childhood homes. But what the hell good is any of that?

Keepsakes are a complete waste of space if you never look at them, no matter where their containers live. And sooner or later, you're going to have to deal with them. (Unless your parents do you the favor of throwing your boxes out when you're not looking. Odds are, you'd never notice.)

Sorry to be blunt, but your parents can't live forever. Sending boxes home to them only delays the inevitable. At least if you deal with your shit now, you're only dealing with what's in front of you. If you wait until you're grieving, those childhood mementos are likely to sit unopened in a storage unit for the rest of your life. Then they become *your* kids' problem. Don't let it get that far. Get it over with now and give your kids the gift of a carefully curated collection of mementos instead of the burden of ten boxes of random crap they don't care about but feel guilty throwing away.

Don't confuse the memory with the thing

True, the second-place ribbon you won at the 4-H fair when you were nine for your handsomely grown spaghetti squash *is* irreplaceable. But no one can take that incredible achievement away from you. So maybe you don't need the ribbon. Maybe the memory is enough. No? Not buying it?

What's the problem here? Do you think you won't remember your big win because you don't have that ribbon handy? Be honest—how often do you actually look at it? Do you even remember it's there if you haven't gone through the bin lately? (If that ribbon is on display somewhere, you may need the help of a good psychiatrist more than a professional organizer.)

In all seriousness, if that ribbon makes you genuinely happy, go ahead and put it somewhere you can see it. But if it's the memory of the day and the resulting winner's ice cream that's making you smile, you don't need the ribbon. I swear to you.

Still on the fence? Consider storing your keepsakes in the cloud rather than in a box in your mother's basement. Designate a folder for pictures of all your mementos, and make sure it's automatically backed up. Upload pictures of all your mementos, then throw the damn things out. You can pull up those pics whenever you feel like taking a walk down Memory Lane—no flight or excavation required.

Keep the crème de la crème

When it comes to the sentimental stuff like greeting cards and old photographs, you can't keep them all. I mean, you *can*. But you're not doing yourself any favors. If you have hundreds of cards and thousands of photos, you're probably not enjoying any of them.

Some people recycle old greeting cards as soon as the holiday or birthday has passed. Be like those people. They get it. They've received and enjoyed the message. The card has served its purpose, and it can happily go in the bin. A lot of greeting cards are made from recycled paper. So really, if you recycle one greeting card, you're giving another one a chance to live. It's the circle of life.

If you're reading this book, you probably feel guilty tossing something that someone lovingly (I hope) chose for you. If you can't join those smart recyclers, then you need to be like a judge at the Westminster Dog Show. Have you seen the way they analyze the dogs and then point to the top contenders? "You. You. Aaaand you." If you're not a decisive person, it's kind of mesmerizing to watch someone be that sure of themselves.

Raise your standards to dog-show levels and choose just one greeting card from each sender to save. Whenever you get a new item from that person, judge it against the one you have. Keep the one that best represents your relationship with that person, then toss the other.

Make sure you take the time to go through and enjoy the cards you save. And if a card really stands out to you, consider framing it and hanging it up. The point is to maximize your enjoyment of your cards, not just leave them in a drawer. If you do that, you may as well recycle them.

Photographic memory not required

Be just as decisive and persnickety with photographs. You probably have photo albums of all shapes, sizes, and levels of decay. Let me tell you a secret: even if they were passed down over the decades, you don't have to hold on to them.

You can take the photos you really love and put them in a new album, then toss the rest.

As cameras and film became cheaper and more accessible, people got a little trigger happy with the shutter button. Not every shot is going to be an Annie Leibovitz, so don't feel bad about tossing the bad ones. The point of a photo album is to tell a story, and sometimes that story could use a good edit.

Do you have 300 photos from your trip to Chincoteague, Virginia? Are 296 of them pictures of horses walking down Main Street? Choose your top three or five and ditch the rest. You don't need them. Every time you look at the remaining photos, the memory of your whole visit will come flooding back. Keep just one album full of standout moments, and you'll enjoy every minute you spend looking through it.

If you're feeling really ambitious, try using this method on the thousands of digital photos clogging up your cloud account. This is no small feat, so I give you full permission to do it over several evenings spent in front of the TV. Just remember how annoying it is to sort through these the next time you get snap-happy with your smartphone.

Another thing to think about is that studies show we

enjoy moments less when we're busy taking photos of them. So consider putting down the camera and really experiencing that gourmet meal/sunset/dolphin sighting. The fewer photos you take, the more memories you make, and the fewer shitty photos you have to sort through.

Collectibles: display them or dump them

Maybe you have boxes of comic books in mint condition, or albums of baseball cards you were sure would be valuable. Or maybe you collected Pogs. (Don't judge me, millennials—they were way cooler than they looked.) But what good is a favorite memento or collectible if it's hidden away in a bin somewhere? Unless you're actively enjoying your collection, there's really no point in having it.

Surrounding yourself with the things you love doesn't mean sitting in the middle of a bunch of bins in the attic once a year. It means proudly displaying those items. If you love your baseball cards, leave the album on your coffee table or frame your favorites. If 12-year-old you loved them but 38-year-old you can live without them, sell or donate them. Don't give me any "I'll get around to selling them" bullshit. Either do it now or donate them.

When is enough enough?

Unfortunately, there is no magical stopping point in your tidying journey. We humans are fickle bastards—you're going to change your mind, change your tastes, buy new things, and get sick of old ones. And all of that can happen right in the middle of organizing your tee shirts. So the truth is, you're never really finished.

That's fine, because I Jedi-mind-tricked you. The point was never to finish tidying. The point was to shift your perspective. By now, you're already feeling lighter. You can look around your home and see things you love, and you know that's how it's supposed to be. You're going to carry that shift with you. It makes you want to keep working on finding what makes you happy in all aspects of your life. (Just don't be an asshole about it at the office— you need those paychecks.)

The process also teaches you to let go of who you used to be and accept who you are right now. That can be tough. It's not just the doe-eyed optimist you used to be in high school. It's also the idiot who impulse-bought a banana-yellow shirt just last week. (How could you have changed your mind so quickly? You know how. Human, remember?)

Appreciate the fact that you've grown—in whatever way that might be—and keep moving forward.

Only you know what your happy place looks like. Have that goal ready in your mind. When you're tempted to say, "This is good enough," compare where you are to where you want to be. Did you get it right? Are you close? Did you lose your way completely? Do you need to tweak the goal to fit with how you've changed along the way? It's all up to you. You're in control. And it feels fucking fantastic.

Your Chapter 3 Checklist

* Start with something so easy it barely takes brain cells
* Keep only the books that make your "desert island" list
* Stop pretending you're going to read any of those dust-covered books
* Empty the fucking magazine basket already
* Switch to paperless statements. Right. Now.
* Stop tearing out recipes your lazy ass is never going to cook and open a Pinterest account instead

* Get your kid used to the idea that not every-thing is art
* Ditch the instruction booklets—you'll wing it or watch it on YouTube
* Make friends with Google drive (scan the important shit, then shred it)
* Stop printing things out!
* Subject the junk drawer to the same scrutiny as your tee shirt collection
* Accept that you'll never be on *The Great British Baking Show* and ditch the mixer
* Stop buying office supplies for the desk you never use—one good pen will do
* Unless you're an Avon lady, you don't need that much fucking makeup
* Sell your DVDs and buy digital movies instead
* Treat your spare change like the cheeseburger it will someday be
* Stop hoarding cardboard boxes
* Accept that you bought way too many sweaters and tees
* Keep the clothes that make you feel awesome when you wear them

* Wear the hot dress you've been saving for a special occasion
* Wear your comfy pants with pride
* Fold your fucking laundry and put it away neatly
* Find a system that works for you and your storage space
* Leave space around your shit so you can actually find it
* Skip the plastic tubs and get rid of enough shit to keep your seasonal stuff handy
* Make some extra time to walk down Memory Lane
* Don't be the asshole who lets your stuff take over your parents' or kids' house
* Take pictures of your keepsakes, then let them go
* Make your greeting cards and photographs compete for the top spot
* Either display those collectibles or squeeze some money out of them
* Keep your happy place in mind as your tastes change

4

Put Sh*t Away

Decide where you want things

You've made it to the fun part! Now you get to find homes for all the things you love and stage your house like you're channeling Joanna Gaines. OK, granted, that might not sound like fun to everyone. Would the promise of a shopping spree at The Container Store make it more appealing? Stay with me. We'll get there.

If you've done the hard work of confronting your clutter and discarding the excess, this part should be a breeze. Hopefully, you've cleared off some shelves, emptied a drawer or two, and saved a little room in your closet. That'll make organizing everything that survived The Culling that much easier. (Don't worry if you haven't—every little bit helps.)

First, pull up that mental picture again and think about how you want the space to feel. (You are both Joanna and the client in this scenario. Feel free to talk amongst yourself.) The trick is to organize what you have left so that it lines up with your vision. Sounds simple enough, right? But it does take some self-awareness.

If you want your bedroom to be as clean and airy as a yoga retreat, you're going to have to rethink that figurine display. Lots of little things in your eyeline create visual clutter and make the space feel more closed in, so maybe you move the figurines to a less restful space. Of course, if you want your home to feel like that cozy little antique store you found on your last road trip through Vermont, the more kitsch the merrier.

This is why it's so important to get clear on what *you* want. I have no one-size-fits-all advice here. I can only give you a little guidance. You have to organize things in a way that makes sense to you and the life you want for yourself.

At this stage, you might find yourself paring down even more while you fine-tune your concept. That's fine—no one said you had to have it all figured out on Day 1. Take your time and make sure you're happy with where things are headed. If you're not, the organization won't stick.

Speaking of which . . . once you've decided where everything will live, you have to make the effort to keep it there. Putting things back where they belong is key to keeping your happy place intact, so it's worth the miniscule amount of effort you need to put in: **Just store things where it makes the most sense. Then, like a good friend after a party, make sure they make it home safe and sound at night.**

Yes, building healthy habits is super annoying. But it's

not like I'm asking you to take up jogging. Have some fucking perspective.

You don't have a lack of storage, you have too much shit

If you half-assed the discard stage, you really screwed yourself. The whole reason you started this project was because you couldn't stand to look at your living space any more. **In case you missed it, throwing your shit in bins doesn't actually help you feel better.**

You spent years bringing things into your life. You have too much stuff. Even if you got rid of half of it, you'd probably still have too much stuff. That's OK—it's a process. But it's one that you really have to dig into. Remember the Michelangelo story? The potential is there, but if you haven't chipped away at the excess, you'll never see it realized.

Here's a little how-to refresher for the lazy assholes who didn't do the work and also don't want to reread Chapter 2: Can't find a good spot for that grade-school trophy? The trash is a viable option. Get over the guilt. Take pictures, recycle or donate what you can, and throw out the rest. You can come back to class once you've caught up.

Bottom line: do not start putting stuff away until you've gotten a handle on all the unnecessary shit in your house. If you get to the point where you're just exhausted and can't sort and discard anymore, take a break and come back to it. But don't just call it quits and shove the stuff under your bed. You know that feeling when your hand is hanging off the bed at night and you suddenly feel the need to pull it up? That's not monsters, it's clutter. Get your shit together and you'll sleep better.

When you've really done the work and you're ready to put things away, take a beat. This is a great time to rearrange furniture that used to be too weighed down with unnecessary crap. Think about whether each piece is working toward what you want before you start filling it up again. You can move some of it around or even get rid of pieces to open up the space. (Just don't go crazy—make sure that the stuff you're keeping still has a place to call home or you'll be back at square one.)

Now that you have the furniture where you want it, you can start to put things away. Imagine your vision for your space is a paint-by-number, and you're just filling it in according to plan. Display things that you love in plain sight and neatly store necessities in drawers and closets, making sure to leave plenty of room around everything. The easier it is to grab what you need, the less likely it is that you'll fuck up your new system in the first week.

Work smarter, not harder

If complex filing systems with labels, tabs, color coding, and indexes float your boat, more power to you. But that's a lot of fucking work for the rest of us. **The best storage systems—the ones you're less likely to fuck up—are the ones that keep things simple.** So don't overthink it.

If you wander into the land of subcategories, you've gone too far. Sorting your bathroom cabinet by skincare and makeup is fine, but sorting your makeup by work, weekend, and "at the club" is a little much. Just throw it all on a shelf with the stuff you use most in the front.

A plastic caddy might be helpful, but it might not. Contrary to popular belief and Pinterest, not everything is made better by being sorted into containers. Socks don't need their own little cubbies. They're socks—they're not going to wander off or get into fights. As long as they're paired up in some way and you can see most of them at a glance, you're fine.

In fact, most things work well undivided in a drawer or sitting on a shelf. If you find you do need a container, check out what you already have. Anything from a shoebox to a honey jar can come in handy if you think about it for a minute.

When you feel yourself getting carried away with storage solutions, follow the yellow brick road back to the beginning and ask yourself WWSD—what would Scarecrow do? He wouldn't bother decanting his cereal into expensive plastic containers, I'll tell you that much. (It already comes in neat rectangular boxes meant to fit on shelves. What more do you want? Buy a chip clip and find other things to worry about.)

I know, I promised you some time at The Container Store. But we're not there yet. **You don't go to TCS for help organizing your shit. You go to TCS for help making it pretty.** So just hang on until you've organized everything and you're ready to make some upgrades. Figure out what you actually want first and make a list. The siren song of TCS, with its aisles of soothingly color-coordinated storage supplies, can crash your bank account if you're not careful.

Keep your shit to yourself

When you're busy living your life, things have a way of wandering from room to room. Your coat has left the closet and now lives on the chair by the door. Your nail polish has made its way from the bathroom to the kitchen table and taken up residence. And you may as well move your laundry basket to the bathroom, because it's not doing you any fucking good in your bedroom.

Hopefully, things started to make their way back to where they came from as you went through the discard phase. You took stock of your storage space, decided where everything would end up, and pared down accordingly. Right? Because a vacation home is one thing, but if your stuff owns more real estate than the Kardashians, you have a whole other problem.

I'm talking to those of you who think it's perfectly normal for your clothing to take over not only the walk-in you share with your partner but also the closets or drawers in other rooms. It's not. You need to take a good, hard look in the mirror. And probably at your credit card statements. You are one person! I repeat, how many fucking sweaters do you need?

Try this: *Your* shit goes in *your* room. Your kids' shit goes in their rooms. Living room shit goes in the living room. See how that works? Unless you live in a studio apartment or you made the Guinness Book of World's Records for world's tiniest closet, there is no fucking excuse for anyone's personal belongings to take over the whole house—especially if you live with other people.

So take another whack at paring down, this time focusing on fitting everything of *yours* in *your* room. The same goes for everyone who lives in the house. Once you have things where they belong, control the creep. Don't let things wander too far from home. **At least once a week, take a look around common areas and other rooms and remove anything that doesn't belong.**

Designating a room for everything and making sure it all stays put helps you tidy up more easily when life and laziness get in the way. You've put all this effort into some stellar sorting and organizing. Don't fuck it up now.

Lean into the lazy

There's nothing wrong with storing things where you use them. You keep the toilet paper in a basket next to the toilet, remote controls next to the couch, and your car keys on a hook by the door. Who doesn't? It makes things easy to grab when you need them and easy to put away when you're done.

The "keep your shit to yourself" rule is meant to help you keep personal items from taking over common areas. If your bedroom isn't where you need something, then ignore the rule. **The goal is to create a living space that works for you, remember?** You're bound to leave certain things lying around anyway, so you may as well incorporate them into your system.

Maybe you keep your wallet or purse on the table by the front door and a pair of shoes under it so you don't have to scramble in the morning. (As someone who simply cannot drag her ass out of bed when the alarm goes off, anything I can do to shave a few seconds off my morning routine is fair game.) Just don't let that one pair of shoes multiply and the table become a dumping ground for receipts, coupons, and spare change. The point is to maximize convenience, and a pile of receipts covering up your car keys and sending you into a foul-mouthed frenzy first thing in the A.M. is the opposite of convenient. (Been there.)

This isn't an excuse to leave random shit scattered all over the house, though. **There's a big difference between storing things where you use them and leaving**

everything lying around within arm's reach. Maybe "random-shit chic" used to be your thing, but you're trying to evolve. Keep things handy but tidy.

You regularly use a spatula in the kitchen, but that doesn't mean it has to sit in a crock on the counter. If you like a clean look, storing it in a drawer by the stove is just as useful (especially if you took my advice and pared down to two). The spatula has a designated place that makes it easy to use and easy to put away, and your countertop doesn't look like a T.J. Maxx. That's a win.

Sometimes storing things where you use them means having the same thing in two places. That's fine. Having a phone charger next to your bed and another one where you sit on the couch is just common sense—especially if you have a phone that's nearing the end of its planned obsolescence. (And we wonder why we're addicted to new and shiny. Hmm . . .)

Storing things where you use them has the added bonus of helping you remember where you put shit. If you've ever wandered from room to room cursing your sunglasses for wandering off (as they do), you'll appreciate having a designated spot for them. Don't worry about storage perfection—worry about living your life.

Pulling out that bottom bin is a bitch

Items on the bottom of piles or stacks are the lost boys of your belongings. If you can't see it, you won't use it. That goes for important papers, clothing that's been shoved to the back of a drawer, and that pancake puff maker you stored under all your baking trays. You may never make pancake puffs again just because you forgot the damn pan existed.

You think your clear plastic totes are any better? A neat stack of bins is just a hot mess in a nice dress. **What are you going to do when you need something from the bottom bin?** The effort involved in extricating it is enough to make you think *I don't really need that*. But if you don't need it, you shouldn't have it. So now you're storing something that either you don't need, or you do need and you're too lazy to use. Awesome.

Stacked or layered storage just doesn't work. **If your lazy ass has any hope of using what you own, it all has to be easy to grab.** Yep, all of it. (OK, you're right. Maybe not all of it. If you put your winter items in a bottom bin, I'm sure that at some point you will get cold enough to do whatever it takes to pull that bin out and get your hands into some mittens. Of course, if your laziness exceeds your willpower, you might just end up buying a new pair, so . . .) Yep, all of it.

The simplest solution is to pare down enough to leave breathing room around all of your belongings. But you can also get creative with the storage you have. **Don't be afraid to think outside the box.** It's your space and you can do whatever the fuck you want with it. (Except stack things inside of it. I think you're with me on that one.)

You were taught that a dresser holds clothes, but deep drawers are the enemy. What if it held shoes and accessories instead? Do you have space in your closet for some folded items? If you don't have a lot of clothing to hang, maybe you can buy one of those hanging fabric things with multiple shelves.

Move things around, try out different solutions, and don't be afraid to get it wrong. Your space is an ever-evolving landscape. Just remember how much fucking work you put into paring down and make sure you have easy access to all of those things you so painstakingly chose to keep.

Channel your inner MacGyver . . . or not

You don't have to spend an entire paycheck on pretty bins—especially if you happen to hoard packaging. Want to finish this project right now? **Cardboard boxes and**

cleaned-out jars are your friends when it comes to storage in a hurry.

You can find all sorts of ways to corral your mess with things you have on hand. Use them to hold everything from cotton balls to garbage bags—anything small or that becomes clutter when left to its own devices. Nestle your collection of Mrs. Meyers dish soaps neatly into a shoebox so they don't get knocked around like bowling pins every time you pull something out of the cupboard under the sink. Stand makeup brushes up in a honey jar (with or without its original "local honey" label intact).

Personally, I'm a big fan of pouches—the ones that come free with purchase or that are meant to store makeup. You usually have a few around the place, and they're a lot more fun and colorful than most containers. Plus, you can fit all sorts of tiny things in them, then tuck them away in a bigger bag or cabinet.

Of course, some things might be better off left alone than shoved into yet another object. Not sure whether you need a box? Try it both ways and choose whatever makes you happier, whether that's smartly arranged bottles of body wash or an old basket that hides them in plain sight.

But . . . I did promise you a chance to roam the aisles of a certain storage and décor store that makes you squeal with delight. **If sturdy boxes covered in decorative fabrics are going to motivate you to get your shit together, your time is now.** Go crazy.

Keep in mind that the "I might need it" rule applies to storage containers, too, so make sure you take your list and keep receipts. Anything you don't use goes back or gets donated. And leftover cardboard boxes and glass jars get put out for recycling. Don't add to your mess just when you're starting to get it sorted out.

Whatever you use, just remember: this is *your* happy place. If you like the Boho feel of organizing with cardboard boxes, then that's what you use. If you want your space to look like Genevieve Gorder designed it, look for chic alternatives. The only person you have to impress is you. Make your space look like the image you've been holding so tightly in your mind for all of these pages.

Russian nesting dolls have their shit together

While you generally don't want to store your stuff in other stuff, you can probably get away with putting a few like items together, turducken style. For example, you can store smaller luggage and travel bags inside of your biggest suitcase, then roll that under the bed or inside the closet. When you need a travel bag, you'll have to pull out the big guy and look at everything he's holding, so it's hard to lose track of any of it.

If you have a few handbags that aren't in rotation, you could probably squeeze them into the luggage nesting doll, too. Or pack them into your largest tote and hang it up somewhere. (Hopefully, you've narrowed down your collection by this point. All you really need is one satchel, one crossbody, and one wristlet in neutral, all-season colors. Save the polka dots and cat whiskers for the wallet.)

Other good candidates for nesting include coats, pans, bakeware, and sheets in their matching pillowcase. **Only nest things if you know it won't get in the way of you knowing they're there and using them.** If you have a super shitty memory, this method might not be for you.

There's one thing we can all use the nesting method for, though. Do you have twenty-three reusable tote bags of varying sizes, colors, and cuteness? They seem to multiply like gremlins, don't they? Whether they came free with purchase, you left yours in the car and had to buy more, or you just couldn't resist the bright red bicycle on that one, you're bound to have more than a few of them. What the hell are you supposed to do with twenty-three reusable totes? Here's an idea: use the fucking things. We only have one planet, people. We have to make it last—at least until we can find another one to fuck up.

Can't seem to remember your totes when you need them? **Stuff all of the totes into the biggest one you have, then hang that one on the doorknob of the door you leave through in the morning.** Store them just like that in your car and you can choose whether to bring the lot for some heavy-duty grocery shopping or just pull one or two like tissues for a quick trip.

Make a concerted effort to keep putting your totes back in your car like this, and to bring them into the stores. If you forget them, walk your lazy ass back out to the car and get them. Once that happens more than a few times, you're either going to start remembering the damn things or you're going to hit your steps. Now not only are you saving the planet, you're getting fit. Come on. Who can't get behind that?

Changing handbags doesn't have to be its own project

Being super organized is great. Being organized to the point of emptying your purse every night and putting away all of its contents, then putting them back in the purse the next day? That's just fucking crazy. And it's a waste of time you could be spending with your kids, or playing *Elder Scrolls* with strangers halfway around the world. **If you want to make it easy to switch handbags, work smarter, not harder.**

I know I'm not the only woman who carries her entire life in her purse. I'll admit, I may be the only one who packs it all into a 10 x 6 x 4-inch space. You would be amazed at all the shit I fit into my little crossbody bag.

My usual haul includes: credit cards, driver's license, AAA card, library card (I walk the walk), and coupons; tissues, mints, hand sanitizer, and hand cream; a small bottle of Excedrin, my migraine meds, Tiger Balm, and ear plugs (you don't want to be caught off-guard with a migraine in a shopping mall); a lip balm, a lip gloss, and a lipstick; a pen and earbuds. Not to mention the phone I shove in there on my way out the door and my keys, which hang from a carabiner while I walk. I was a Girl Scout. I am prepared for the Zombie Apocalypse—if the zombies get migraines or need to write something down.

When I use a larger purse, I break out some pretty little pouches that I can move from one bag to another

without having to empty their contents. You can put lip products and mints in one, cords and earbuds in another, pens and headache meds in a third. Use a coin purse or credit card wallet for coupons and store-specific cards so they don't clutter up your everyday money. When you're ready to change bags, you just move a few pouches instead of dozens of small items. You'll be itching to use those pockets, but leave them for easy-grab items like your phone, sunglasses, and keys.

Choosing the right bag helps. My little one has credit card slips so I don't need a wallet, and a few pockets to help keep things sorted. But it's still a hell of a lot for a very small bag. If I had to take it all out every night just to put it all back every day, I'd probably cry myself to sleep. There's just no fucking reason for it.

American closets are not one-size-fits-all

Around here, you can drive around a single neighborhood and see thirty-five different kinds of architecture and homes of all shapes and sizes. Maybe you have five walk-ins, or maybe you have one tiny recess. Maybe you have built-in storage, or maybe one rickety wooden pole. This makes organizing a little easier for some than for others. **You just have to make do with what you've got.**

Ideally, you have a linen closet for sheets, towels, and toiletries; a bedroom closet for clothes and shoes; and a hall closet for coats and miscellaneous shit like golf clubs and umbrellas. If you do, you should have no problem putting everything away neatly and with plenty of space around all of it. If you're Mr. Five Walk-In Closets, I expect your home to look like an ad for IKEA storage solutions. No excuses.

If you don't have quite as much space, you're just going to have to get creative. Maybe you need to seriously consider a capsule wardrobe. Or maybe you have some room to spare and just buy a bigger dresser. Only you know how much shit you have after your purge and whether it will fit in the storage you've got.

The hard part might be making your lack of storage line up with your vision for a clean space. If that's the case, there are a few tricks you can try. Add shelving to a simple closet with a hanging closet organizer or two. Create hanging space for longer items with over-the-door hooks. You can hang these hooks on both sides of a closet door to maximize storage, or just on the inside if you want a cleaner look.

Do you have a standard bed (of any size) with four feet? Buy some bed risers from your local home store. These are rubber feet you can put under each corner of your bed to lift it a few inches and make it easier to reach underneath it. (Bonus: you feel like royalty crawling into a bed that's a few inches higher up. Add a down comforter and some throw pillows for the full effect.)

For a totally clean look, add a bed skirt that suits your taste. Gray and tailored, pink and ruffled—it doesn't matter, as long as it makes you happy and hides your extra shit. Store things in wheeled under-bed bins, which give you easy access to your hidden storage. Just make sure you get the kind with the hinged lid. You can pull these out halfway from either side of the bed and easily lift the top completely to see what you have.

Whatever storage solutions you come up with, make sure everything is still accessible. You didn't go through all of this shit to forget you have that killer cocktail dress. You want that thing in plain view so you remember to grab it for brunch with the gang. (Create your occasion, remember?)

If you can see it, it should make you happy

This one's easy enough: show off the things you love and store the necessities and backups. Once again, you have to decide what makes you happy and where you want those things to live. I can't decide for you.

When you find yourself overthinking things, try to tap into your common sense. I know it's not easy for everyone, but stay with me. Should the toilet plunger be sitting out next to the toilet, or should you tuck it into or behind something? Well, you have to ask yourself: Do you enjoy looking at the toilet plunger?

If the answer is no, you tuck the plunger way. But I don't know your story. Maybe you fell in love with your neighbor when he helped you unclog your toilet, so the plunger holds a happy memory. Everyone's different. Personally, I probably would have moved. But I have a low threshold for embarrassment.

Occasionally, things you don't love have to sit out where you use them. But that doesn't mean you have to look at them. If your cluster of shampoo and body wash bottles doesn't make you happy, close the fucking shower curtain. Problem solved.

And if your shower curtain doesn't make you happy, it's time to go shopping. Those things are like $14 and can make a huge difference in your mood when you're going through the motions in the morning.

Once you've decided which of your belongings deserve the spotlight, you have to choose the stage. **Take a leaf out of *HGTV*'s book and use your open shelving units for more than storage.** A bookcase or a tabletop can feature an elegant mix of favorite books, picture frames, and flower vases. Display your items in a way that makes you smile.

The key is leaving some breathing room around your favorite items so that they really shine. And to keep yourself from using these displays as an excuse to clutter shit up again. That one's important.

Embrace the embarrassing shit

Just because you're an adult now doesn't mean you can't show off your nerdy collectibles. If you're self-conscious, you could set up a special shelf or drawer hidden away from guests who won't get it. But again, it's your fucking house, and it's supposed to make you happy. You don't see your boring friends apologizing for playing Kenny G during dinner. (Their home, their food, their smooth jazz.) **Do not apologize for geeking out in your own home.**

If turning your home into your happy place makes you want to wallpaper the living room in Marvel posters, go for it. But if you want to feel like a grown-up *and* express yourself, chart some middle course. Strive for something along the lines of *nerd chic*.

You could frame three of your favorite superhero posters and hang them on the wall behind the couch. Leave a few figurines strategically placed on your shelves among those books and picture frames we talked about. Tuck your Nintendo into your TV console and your games into a drawer, but leave an Amiibo or two out on display.

You're lucky enough to be living in the Age of the Nerds, so take advantage of it. Fancy-pants home décor and kitchen brands Pottery Barn and Williams Sonoma both have collections dedicated to *Harry Potter*. You can't throw a rock without hitting something emblazoned with themes from *Star Wars* or *Legend of Zelda*. In other words, you have plenty of options for incorporating your geekdom into your tastefully organized home.

Just keep checking in with your mental picture to make sure you're not overdoing it. A gallery wall of framed *Alice in Wonderland* quotes and illustrations interspersed with mirrors could be cute. Turning your living room into the Mad Hatter's tea party may be a little much. But you do you.

Live like your mother-in-law's stopping by

Keeping things tidy should be its own reward, right? So should eating healthy, but if you're not dropping pounds on the scale or lowering your blood pressure, you're bound to think *Fat lot of good those fucking salads are doing me* before you down a cheeseburger as retribution. **We humans are lazy, and it takes some serious effort to change our habits. Sometimes, we need some extra motivation.**

Have you ever let the FedEx guy think no one was home—despite the car in the driveway and the TV blaring—because you just woke up and looked like hell? Or because you hadn't vacuumed the cat hair off the living room floor in more than a week? Even when we truly don't give a shit what other people think, we still freak out a little when strangers get a glimpse of how we live.

Back in the day, unexpected guests were a welcome surprise met with coffee cake. Today, a knock at the door inspires anxiety and suspicion. **Wouldn't it be great if the state of your living room didn't add to your desire to hit the deck at the sound of the doorbell?** Keep shit clean, and it won't.

Do you have an overstepping mother-in-law, or a nosey neighbor you can't stand? Every night, before you're so exhausted that you have to zombie-walk to your bed, take a look around. Would you be fine with how things look if that person stopped by bright and early tomorrow morning? You've been busy, so probably not.

Take five minutes to tidy up the living room, powder room, and kitchen—basically, anywhere your mother-in-law could get to in a five-minute visit. Use a basket to gather up anything that doesn't belong and put it in your room. Your room is a free zone. If anyone goes in there without your permission, they are operating way outside the bounds of human etiquette and their opinion is basically void.

When you have a little more time, or when the basket starts to overflow, put some effort into doing a real cleanup. Don't stop until the basket is empty and ready to be filled with the results of tonight's five-minute tidy.

Clutter in organization's clothing

Don't let some attractive storage fool you into thinking you have your shit together. It's too easy to get a bunch of pretty bins from a home store and dump everything you own in them. Yes, they look really tidy lined up like that in the closet. But can you find what you need when you need it? Did you really organize everything, or did you end up tossing some homeless items in with other things?

If you love the clean look of those bins, by all means, keep using them. **But attractive storage isn't an excuse to half-ass all of the hard work of sorting and organizing.** You may as well have no-assed it for all the good it's doing you. For those bins to be doing their job, they need to contain neatly arranged items of a particular type or category.

Three bins in a linen closet that hold a hodgepodge of toiletries, cleaning supplies, Command strips, extension cords, light bulbs, Duct tape, and period supplies are going to cause nothing but frustration. Three bins in a linen closet that hold folded washcloths, extra toilet paper, and guest toiletries respectively keep the overall system simple and the items easy to access. There's a big difference.

Worse yet is using bins and baskets out in the open to hold everything you didn't feel like finding a real,

permanent home for. A lovely wicker basket here and there says, "I read *Better Homes & Gardens*." Baskets full of magazines, shoes, remote controls, towels, toiletries, cleaning supplies, and other miscellaneous crap lining the floors and countertops say, "I don't have a fucking clue what else to do with this stuff."

Instead of putting two remotes in a tiny basket on the coffee table, stuff the Blu-ray player remote you don't use into a cupboard and leave the universal remote out. I promise you won't miss the basket or the Blu-ray remote.

Be grateful, not guilt-ridden

If you surround yourself with things that you love, you're bound to be grateful for them. And that in itself is going to create a shift in your life. **Now that you've trained yourself to spot what makes you happy, you'll easily find more to love.** You'll start being more mindful about your purchases, and you'll be more careful with the things you own.

You used to take a more *Game of Thrones* approach to laundry—toss it all in and see what survives. But now that sweater in your hands isn't just one of a few dozen sweaters you own. It's the berry pink sweater that makes you feel amazing when you wear it. So you're going to launder it properly, damn it. And you're not going to throw it on the floor when it's dirty, or fuck it up with spills or tears. Because you appreciate that sweater.

And appreciating your belongings is great. **But there's a big difference between being grateful for what you have (à la Oprah) and anthropomorphizing inanimate objects.** One helps you feel satisfied with your life, the other gives you stomach pains every time you think about throwing something out. If you want something you can feel good about sweet-talking, try a potted plant.

More often than not, something will happen to that sweater. The cat will rip a hole in it trying to get away from you, or you'll just wear the thing out after a while. You don't want to freak out, thinking you've disappointed the sweater. You also won't want to admit that an item has seen better days because you'll feel guilty about putting it out to pasture (a.k.a. throwing it in the trash). But if the item really is worn out, that's the only place for it.

Think of your guilt like a cold . . . you do your best to deal with it and not pass it along to others. Resist the temptation to donate your worn-out items as a last-ditch effort to "do right by" them. By all means, be thankful for your things. And be sad when you have to throw them out. But don't treat them like they have feelings unless you want to feel shitty every time you piss off the cat or your tastes change.

Your Chapter 4 Checklist

* Find a home for all the shit you're keeping
* If you can't find a home for everything, you have too much shit—try again
* Don't outsmart yourself with complicated storage systems
* Stop letting your shit escape and hold other rooms hostage
* Store things where you use them
* Don't stack things unless you never plan on using whatever's at the bottom
* Find containers that make you as happy as the things you're storing
* Store shit inside other, similar shit (as long as you'll remember you did it)
* Use pouches and card wallets to simplify switching handbags
* Make do with the storage you have
* Give your stuff some breathing room

* Put the stuff you love in plain sight and tuck the other shit away
* Let your home reflect who you are, however nerdy
* Live like strangers are going to see your messy bathroom and judge you
* Don't use bins and baskets as an excuse to have more shit than you should
* Do not treat inanimate objects like living things if you want to retain your sanity

5

The Magical Feeling of Having Your Sh*t Together

Become a decision-making badass

Whittling your house down to just the things you love takes balls. You've made decision after decision based on your own internal compass. You should feel ready to take on the fucking world right now!

One of the hardest things a person can do is figure out what they want. We're so programmed to please other people, play by society's rules, and dutifully climb the ladder. Finding the real you beneath all of those expectations takes a lot of introspection and hard work. And that's what you've been doing this whole time.

Throughout the tidying process, you've decided on what makes you happy, what isn't working for you, what is working for you, where to put things, and how you want to use your living space. A mere mortal may have been overwhelmed, but not you! You just took it one step at a time, mastering new skills like a boss.

Think about how handy these skills are and how you can use them going forward. **Not only will you be able to wrangle any unnecessary shit that tries to worm its way into your home, but you'll take a lot less shit outside of your home.** You know what you want. You do what it takes to get it. So what now?

A better job with a boss who respects your opinion? A supportive partner who feels like a best friend? A house of your own so that you can put down roots and not worry about your security deposit every time the cat throws up on the rented carpet? You know what you need to do: figure out what you want, hold a picture of it in your mind, take one little step at a time toward creating it, and adjust as necessary.

And you know that you can do it, because you already have. You're Harry Potter at the *end* of *The Prisoner of Azkaban*. You've seen yourself do the impossible, and it gives you the strength to do it again. So now that you've gotten your shit together, what are you going to do next?

Make room in your life for more good stuff

How to let go is one of the hardest lessons for us to learn. We have to say goodbye to people and pets we love, jobs we maybe hated but needed, bad friends we thought were good friends, and each season of our lives as it gives way to the next. Maybe that's why we hold on so tightly to our stuff.

Theoretically, we could keep our belongings forever—long after the technology is obsolete or the fabric is worn out. We never need to let go if we don't want to. But that's a really fucking limited way to live, isn't it? (I hope you're nodding along and not hoarding a pile of old, worn-out socks you can't bear to throw out.)

Letting go can be devastating, but it can also bring you more happiness than you can imagine. Getting rid of the bad (or even mediocre) shit means the good shit takes center stage. If you've gone through the process, you should have a home that lights you up inside. That alone is worth the work. But it's not the only benefit.

When you hone your vision for your life and you get rid of the shit that isn't working, you make room for better things, people, and opportunities. It's like that friend you have who went through a bad breakup and thought she'd never love again, and then her future husband walks through the door of the coffee shop. If she hadn't gotten rid of the asshole boyfriend (whom you never liked, by the way), she wouldn't have been available to meet the love of her life.

You have to clear a path for the good to come in and stand out. That goes for everything in life, from clothing and toiletries to friends and jobs. Having mastered the art of letting go in your tidying project, you know how strong and prepared you are to pave the way in other aspects of your life. So don't be afraid to unfriend the jackass who keeps blowing you off or quit that shitty job with the toxic boss. Better things will come when you open yourself up to them.

A clean space helps you hit the reset button

Between annoying coworkers, know-it-all clients, and asshole drivers, it's all you can do to drag yourself through your front door and onto the couch. The last thing you want to do is come home to a clusterfuck of a living situation. The point of all this hard work is to have a home that feels like coming up for air.

Whenever you feel resistant about the process or just too lazy to do the fucking work, think about the endgame. Imagine how you'll feel coming home to a space that's organized and filled with things that you love. Then think about how you feel about coming home now.

Does the overflowing closet fill you with dread? Is the laundry basket a permanent fixture in your bedroom? Is it nearly impossible to find anything you're looking for? Have you just become accustomed to only seeing small areas of flooring beneath all of the crap you just can't deal with?

Final question: When is enough enough? You can't keep living like this. Your home is probably the one place you have any control. You can't control your boss or your clients, you can't control the other cars on the road, and you can't control the fact that they've discontinued your favorite cereal. But you *can* control whether you have neatly organized drawers with just the right amount of clothing, or a closet that seems to have projectile-vomited onto your bedroom floor.

Get your shit together at home and you can take back control of your life. **Once you've finished the process of purging and organizing, your home will be a place where you can recharge your batteries.** Refreshed from a night in your happy place, you'll greet the next day without the baggage of everything that came before it.

I'm not saying you'll start loving your customer service job, but you'll certainly have an easier time of smiling in the face of bullshit. And you'll start to find more ways outside of your home to bring happiness into your life. So in a way, tidying is better for you than a meditation practice. (Maybe do some meditation, too. Just to hedge your bets.)

Tidying is like therapy you don't have to pay for

Some people shop to fill a void, because happiness lies just ahead, in that shiny new KitchenAid mixer. Others hoard hotel toiletries because they don't want to be wasteful. Whatever your reasons for bringing shit into your home and holding on to it, you're going to have to deal with them head-on. No one is going to do it for you.

As you build up your "fuck it" muscles by deciding what stays and what goes, you're really learning to process the reasons for your clutter. At first, you resist. You find excuses for keeping things you don't want or need, like "I might use it someday" or "This was a gift." But excuses won't get you to your happy place, so you have to learn to call bullshit on yourself.

When you feel yourself resisting, explore the real reasons. Maybe you realize that you're holding on to that piggy bank from your childhood because you think your dad will be disappointed in you for getting rid of something he gave you. But if you asked your dad, he probably wouldn't give a damn. Clearly that's more about you and how you perceive your relationship with him than it is about him. Deep, right?

If you look hard enough, you'll find all sorts of psychological crap lurking among the tangible crap. You're human. You've spent some years on this plant. You're bound to have some baggage. But through the process of tidying up, you're learning to ID it, process it, and get past it. You're going to break some bad habits and clear out old patterns of thought, which can only help you.

Technically, the therapy isn't free. You've already paid for retail therapy, buying all the crap you're now tossing. And if you don't learn your lesson, you'll just keep paying for it. You're better off if you put some elbow grease into dealing with your shit before things get really expensive.

Sometimes you're going to regret tossing the toaster

More often than not, you won't miss the items you ousted. Other times, you'll need to remind yourself why they got the boot. And sometimes, you need to buy a fucking toaster because the toaster oven makes crappy toast but awesome pizza. You thought you didn't need both, but you do. And you know what? You like the new toaster better than the one you tossed, because it has the little snowflake button for freezer items.

That little one-act play is how regret goes down after a tidying spree. As long as you're not tossing one-of-a-kind antiques that will bring you millions of dollars when they're discovered in the attic under the old board games, you're not going to regret getting rid of shit. Seriously.

Think about it in terms of your spice rack. You want to make a special dish, so you buy some cumin. But cumin isn't part of your regular repertoire, so years go by and you never use it again. When you realize it's expired, you throw it out. No biggie. Then someone gives you a recipe for a dinner they made and you loved, and it requires cumin. Do you have a hissy fit because you threw yours away? No. You go to the store and buy some damn cumin. While you like to think that most of your stuff is irreplaceable, more often it's like cumin.

Not only is your extra shit unnecessary and taking up usable space, it's also giving you anxiety. If you feel like you have to hold on to stuff so that you're always prepared, you can never relax. But when you regret tossing something and then find another solution, you realize that letting go isn't that serious. Most of what you keep "just in case" can be easily replaced with a quick trip to Walmart.

And usually the new item is an upgrade. Suddenly, your anxiety starts giving way to confidence.

As you go through your belongings, you're supposed to ask yourself if you like them, if you need them, and if they can be easily replaced. When you're having trouble letting go of a particular item, add one more question to the list: What's the worst that can happen if I toss it? Usually, the worst-case scenario is nothing more than a mild inconvenience.

Dress like you're ready to get your hands dirty

Ironically, tidying isn't a tidy process. **You're going to be elbow deep in stuff that may not have seen the light of day for several years.** That means encountering some dust, dirt, and bugs, not to mention the occasional mysterious liquid. You're welcome to wear whatever makes you happy, but as a person who's accident prone, I like to err on the side of caution.

I prefer a good, thick pair of already-ruined jeans (splattered with paint or stained with grease from who knows what) and a long-sleeve tee to start. Sneakers are a must, especially if I'm going to be working in the garage or with heavy shit I could drop on my feet. Any place that might be home to arachnids automatically involves garden gloves. Just thinking about one of their furry little feet touching bare skin is enough to make me run screaming from the building, so I take precautions.

Arm yourself with whatever tools you need for a long session of sorting—bottle of water, snacks, a broom to chase off any snakes or mice living in the attic. Think I'm kidding? Be careful when you move things. You never know who has taken up residence in the nooks and crannies you've created with all that excess crap. (Did you need more incentive to get rid of shit? You're welcome.)

Keep a vacuum and a duster handy so you can clean as you go. You might never find that pile of dust again if you go looking for it (probably because you're trying hard not to look for it). After you've finished discarding and before you put things away is a good time to spray for any bugs if they're an issue for you.

Is that whining I hear? Get over it. You know that phrase "It's a dirty job, but someone's got to do it"? That someone is you. This is your mess, and you are responsible for cleaning it up. I repeat, leaving it for someone else to clean up after you die is a dick move.

How do you want your home to feel?

At this point, you've gone through the whole process, or at least the whole book. (If you haven't, you're missing some good shit. Go back and try again. I'll wait right here.) I'll ask you again: How do you want to feel in your home? Think about what popped into your head the first time I asked you that. Where are you now? Has the picture changed?

Have you been able to achieve what you set out to achieve? If not, what's stopping you? One thing that could be getting in your way is that you haven't gotten to the heart of what you want. You look at a picture of a house staged by Joanna Gaines and think *That's what I want*. But what is it about that space? Is it something specific, like the farmhouse décor? The light colors? The earthy wood furniture? The giant clock? Or is it something more—the openness, the brightness, the homey feeling?

A vibe is certainly more difficult to replicate than an object (which you can probably buy from Joanna's website for a small fortune). But it's usually the vibe we're after. That's why you have to stop worrying about what your happy place looks like and start thinking about what it feels like. Then identify other things that make you feel that way.

If you want to surround yourself with Zen-like energy, then clean lines and clear floors are a must. (And maybe an orchid. Zen spaces always seem to have orchids. And river rocks.) If you want your space to feel like a country cottage, soft surfaces and flowers are a start. (Fake flowers are fine, if you tend to kill living things.)

Scroll through pics of homes on Pinterest and practice assigning a feeling to each. Try to figure out what the ones you like have in common. Your home is like a mirror, reflecting back to you what you put into it. If you don't figure out what you really want from the space, you're never going to create a home that makes you happy.

Your home has to evolve with you

You've climbed the mountain, finished the marathon, crossed the Channel! Are you ready to do it again? If you just told me to fuck off, I don't blame you. Sorting through a lifetime of shit is no small feat. No one wants to think about having to do it more than once.

But we humans are complicated creatures. Not only do

we adapt to what's going on in our lives, we also just evolve at random. **If you want your home to keep making you happy, you're going to have to do a little upkeep from time to time.**

As long as you haven't half-assed the work, this should become automatic. Maybe you'll internalize the process so much that you'll just notice when something stops making you happy and take care of it. Or maybe you need to stop and take stock every so often, scheduling mini purges in your calendar.

Don't feel guilty when your tastes change (and they will) and you suddenly hate the comforter that you were in love with just months ago. Instead, embrace the opportunity to prune just a little more. Find new things that make you smile and donate the old ones. There's nothing wrong with fine-tuning your happy place.

Just don't let yourself backslide. You're your own worst enemy and your only superhero. If things start to get cluttered or you continue buying shit you don't need, you're going to have to kick your own lazy ass. You might need to skim this book for a refresher, or you might need to remind yourself that you didn't do all that fucking work just to fall back into old, unhappy habits.

Always keep that mental picture of your happy place

handy. Turn it into something tangible if you need to, whether that's a Pinterest board or just a paragraph on a piece of scrap paper. Update it whenever things change. Just keep making your happiness a priority and your living space will follow suit.

Whenever possible, give old things new life

Even if you can't remember why, you spent good money on that stuff you're about to toss. One way of showing gratitude and respect for those items is to donate them to local charities. That way, even the bad decisions become good ones.

Whether you sell your stuff, you donate it, or you recycle it, there are plenty of ways to win karmic brownie points and assuage the heaping helping of guilt that comes with living in a fast-fashion world. You'd be surprised at how much of your old, ugly, and worn-out stuff can be put to good use.

Want your stuff to go where it's needed most? Optometry offices usually accept old pairs of glasses, which go to people who can't afford them. And a quick Google search can help you find programs that will reformat donated cell phones and give them to soldiers, low-income families, victims of domestic abuse, and kids in need.

Clothing and household goods can be used to support any number of local and national charities, from Habitat for Humanity to the women's shelter up the street. You could dump your stuff at the nearest donation box (of which there are many) or choose to support a cause that speaks to you. The charities might use your goods directly, or they may sell them at a thrift store and use the proceeds. You may have to make peace with seeing a stranger wearing the bedazzled jean jacket your ex-boyfriend gave you. Better them than you.

At the very least, just make sure your shit doesn't end up in a landfill. Recycling stations at stores like Best Buy and IKEA make it easy to get rid of plastics, paper, batteries, light bulbs, and all sorts of electronics without the guilt.

There's also a new kid on the block called Terracycle. This company is on a mission to recycle literally everything, from candy wrappers to used gum. Better than its ending up as a million black spots on concrete, right? (Maybe I take back what I said about people evolving.) They also partner with major brands to make more sustainable packaging, which in turn makes recycling easier for everyone.

Sometimes, the choice is out of your hands. Don't hang on to things just because they're too far gone to donate. Either throw them out or upcycle them yourself into something you'll use. (Those vintage tees from your years as an Aerosmith groupie would look pretty fucking amazing framed or sewn into a throw blanket.)

Clutter messes with your shit

If you think that stubbing your toe on your nightstand after tripping over the clean laundry you have piled on your floor is the worst clutter has to offer, you've got another thing coming. That shit invades every aspect of your health and well-being. The sooner you get your shit together, the better off you'll be.

How, you ask? **Studies show that clutter negatively affects your creativity, productivity, and mental health.** Think about it. How many times have you had to stop what you were working on to riffle through the papers on your desk? Or lost paperwork entirely and had to suffer the consequences (having to redo work you've already done, or worse, your boss making you and your mess her pet project)?

When you lose something, do you coolly sort through your things until you find what you need? Or do you panic and toss the place, like the leader of a pyramid scheme who hears the Feds breaking down the door? That stress is no joke, and it's completely unnecessary. If you have your shit together, the only thing you need to worry about is your coworker microwaving his tuna melt.

Even if you think you work best amid organized chaos, you don't. **A desk covered in piles of papers and half-eaten power bars automatically makes your brain twitchy.** Spend an afternoon clearing things off and you're going to notice a difference.

You might also notice an uptick in your physical health. Dust, allergens, dirt, mold, and bacteria can all hide around and cling to clutter. Tidy up your shit, clean the now-clear surfaces, and you'll be able to breathe a hell of a lot easier.

But that's not all, Bob! **Besides your sanity, creativity, productivity, and lung capacity, you'll also win . . . a healthy savings account!** How do you think that clutter is working for your wallet? When you can't find something small or replaceable, what do you usually do? You buy a new one. Those lost ear buds add up.* How about when you lose an important document and have to pay for a copy? Do you know how much a new birth certificate costs? You don't want to find out. Get your shit together so you don't have to.

Don't let your shopping history repeat itself

Now that you've got your home looking and feeling the way you want, be mindful of the new stuff you bring in and how it fits with your little oasis. You have to unlearn the habits taught to you by advertising executives and the convenience of online shopping. **Stop. Buying. Shit. You. Don't. Need. That may be the most important lesson you could learn from this book.**

Think you've found a loophole in freebies? Nope. If you're one of those assholes who reads between the lines when it benefits them: stop *bringing home* shit you don't

---

* If you have the fancy wireless kind, you better treat those things like your firstborn. That's just too much money to lose just for being a lazy clusterfuck of a person.

need. Just say No to gifts, promo materials, and other people's crap.

You're going to have to do a shopping detox if you really want to break the habit. Unsubscribe from store emails. Avoid the malls. Make a list of what you need and only buy what's on the list. Mull things over. Treat stores like art galleries—you have to *really* love something to spend the money and "hang" it in your house. Most importantly, find other ways to spend your time. Take a walk, get a massage, go for drinks with friends. Just don't go shopping.

But what if you get dragged into Pier 1 against your will and the canvas print you've just spotted makes you deliriously happy? Well, how many times have you bought something that you were totally in love with in the store only to feel meh about it when you got it home? The best way to test the waters is to visit an item several times before you buy it. Don't worry—it'll be there for a while. And if it's not, thank your tidying angels for intervening.

This is not a situation where you'll regret the things you did not do. You're not going to be lying there on your death bed, wishing you had bought that new 4K smart TV. (That thing will be $300 cheaper two months from now when they come out with a better model, and then you'll be pissed that you got a raw deal.)

Very rarely will you regret *not buying* something. Just look at your discard pile to see how often you regret *buying* something. So take some time. Put some space between you and the thing you want. If you still want it after a few weeks (maybe months for the big stuff), then you can buy it. Just don't think twice about donating the thing and eating the money if you don't love it a few months from now. You enjoyed having it (at least for a minute), and you'll enjoy your space even more when it's gone.

Life after clutter

I'm willing to bet that "organize the fucking house" has been first on your to-do list for a long time—and that it never gets checked off. Now imagine that it's done. **What are you going to do now that the house is in order and you've got these badass decision-making skills?** What's next for you?

Life can really kick your ass, but you've got a whole new arsenal of coping mechanisms for dealing with it: Don't think twice before getting rid of something that doesn't work for you. Just keep ignoring the shoulds and holding yourself accountable for creating the life you want.

Surround yourself with things that light you up, and carry that light with you through your day.

Never stop honing those skills and exercising your "fuck it" muscles. You think they were helpful with getting your shit together at home? Wait until you try them out at work, or at the next family reunion. Aunt Carol isn't going to know what hit her when she starts in on you about settling down.

You've worked hard for those "fuck it" muscles. Remember what this place looked like before? Remember how difficult it was to let go in the beginning? But it was worth it. Take a look around at your awesomely organized house, your own personal happy place. Stop to appreciate what you've done and how you feel now. It wasn't elves. It was you. **You're the magic.**

Your Chapter 5 Checklist

* Use your ninja-like decision-making skills for good
* Clear out the bad so that the good stands a fucking chance of getting in
* Turn your home into a little oasis from life's bullshit
* Deal with your shit head on

* Loosen your death grip on anything you can get at Walmart
* Dress like you're heading into battle (which you are)
* Remember what you wanted when you started this project
* Give your vision a little room to grow
* Always try to sell, donate, or recycle shit before throwing it out
* Clear the clutter and save yourself
* Stop. Buying. Shit. You. Don't. Need.
* Pat yourself on the back for getting your shit together